English Looking-glasses

English Looking-glasses

A Study of the Glass, Frames and Makers (1670–1820)

GEOFFREY WILLS

FOREWORD BY JOHN HAYWARD
Deputy Keeper of the Department of Woodwork,
Victoria and Albert Museum

COUNTRY LIFE LIMITED

2–10 TAVISTOCK STREET COVENT GARDEN LONDON

First published in 1965
by Country Life Ltd
2–10 Tavistock Street, London WC2
Printed in Great Britain
by Hazell Watson & Viney Ltd
Aylesbury, Bucks

© Geoffrey Wills 1965

Contents

List of Plates

Foreword

BY JOHN HAYWARD,
Deputy Keeper of the Department of Woodwork, Victoria and Albert Museum

ENGLISH looking-glass frames have long attracted the admiration which is their due, but though a number of brief accounts of their development have been written, there has hitherto been no monograph devoted exclusively to them. It would be difficult to find anyone more competent to undertake the first full-scale work on the subject than Mr Geoffrey Wills, whose detailed researches into almost every field of the applied arts have brought so much new and valuable information to light.

Mr Wills's book contains more than the title indicates, for it deals not only with frame design but with every aspect of the subject, including methods of manufacture. It includes a great deal of information based on original unpublished research, particularly in the list of makers which constitutes the final section. This is, in fact, no mere list of names, for it displays a remarkable knowledge of the source material of the period, including contemporary newspapers and journals.

The period covered by the book is not a long one. The earliest identifiable English looking-glasses were not made before the mid-seventeenth century and looking-glass design suffered the same decline as the other applied arts during the second quarter of the nineteenth century. The subject, on the other hand, is not easy to master. English looking-glasses were more international in style than other types of furniture and careful study is required in order to distinguish between some English and Continental examples. But it is a most rewarding study. In English looking-glass design the Rococo style found its most vivid expression, while it was on the frames of looking-glasses, and on the pier or console tables which accompanied them, that some of the finest English carving of the eighteenth century was lavished.

Author's Preface

THIS book deals with the wall-glasses made in England approximately between the years 1670 and 1820, and describes not only the actual glass and how it was made but the patterns of the frames as they changed in the course of time. Much information, some of it fresh and hitherto unpublished, is given about the careers and work of the men who designed, made and sold these looking-glasses; especially those who lived during the eighteenth century when the design and workmanship of frames were of a particularly high standard. The glass itself was then often imported, but by the end of the century large-scale production had been started here, and this developed sufficiently to supply the home market as well as to provide a surplus for export.

A great debt is due to the late Mr R. W. Symonds for his pioneer work on the subject, and to Mr Peter Ward-Jackson, whose publication of a selection of eighteenth-century furniture designs has whetted the appetite of every keen student of the subject. It is to be hoped that it will be possible, at some future date, to print more of the hitherto unpublished work of Lock, Chippendale, Linnell and others. Such a course would be of incalculable help to all who are interested in looking-glass frames, and in English furniture in general.

Acknowledgement is made to Her Majesty Queen Elizabeth II for gracious permission to reproduce photographs of pieces at Windsor Castle and Hampton Court, and to the other owners of looking-glasses who have kindly allowed them to be used as illustrations.

G. W.

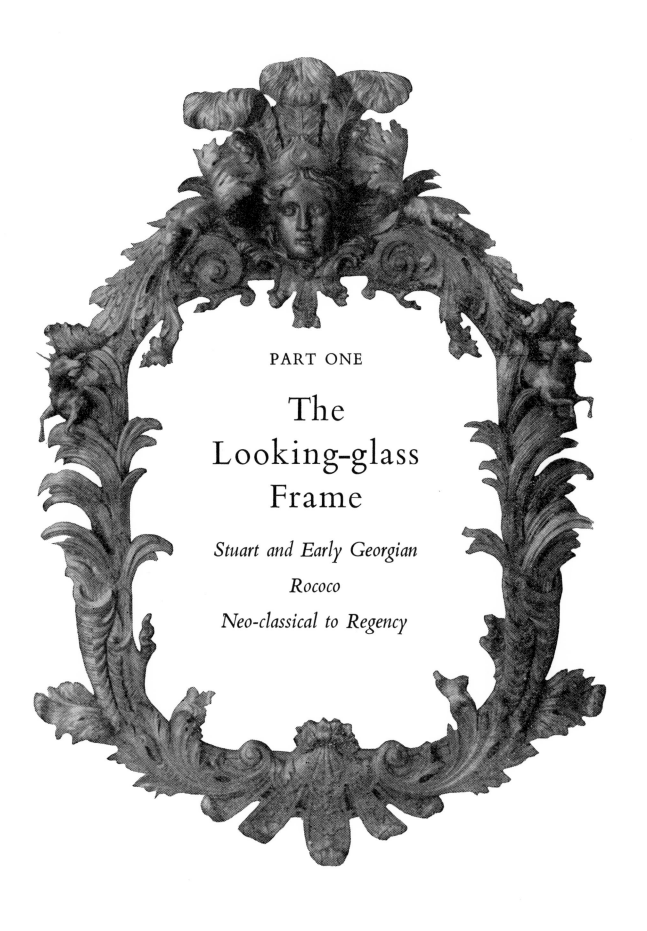

PART ONE

The Looking-glass Frame

Stuart and Early Georgian

Rococo

Neo-classical to Regency

I

Stuart and Early Georgian

THE history of the looking-glass throughout the world is interwoven with tales of wonder mixed with fear and superstition. Man-made reflectors were preceded for many thousands of years by the natural surface of still water; a surface recorded in mythology in the punishment of Narcissus. Primitive man thought that the reflection of a person, like his shadow, represented the soul, and if allowed to rest on water it would be dragged below and drowned by water-spirits. The soul of the innocent native was no less vulnerable in any man-made reflector, when land-based spirits would hasten to carry off the precious projection. The old custom of covering the looking-glass in a sick-room is explained in similar terms, for, during illness, the soul was liable to leave the stricken body more easily than usual and to permit a reflection of the invalid would be hazardous. Furthermore, the soul was supposed not to part company with the body of a dead person until burial, and for the same reason any looking-glasses in a house were covered until after the funeral.

These and other superstitions diminished in strength and frequency with advancing civilisation, but the looking-glass even today embodies a number of long-standing legends and beliefs, and is a reminder of the narrow division between past and present. Such traditions help to explain why it has always been accorded esteem, and to these have been added the high cost and the fragility of the actual glass. It is little wonder that framing has been carried out usually with an elaboration involving both artistic imagination and financial expenditure commensurate with such an exotic.

There are a number of records of looking-glasses in England in the sixteenth century, but no examples have survived and it is probable that all were brought from abroad. Descriptions do not mention the origin of examples, but often give an idea of their appearance. Paul Hentzner, for instance, who visited London in 1598 as tutor to a young German nobleman, wrote: 'We were shown, at the house of Leonard Smith, a taylor, a most perfect looking-glass, ornamented with gold, pearl, silver, and velvet, so richly as to be estimated at five hundred ecus du soleil', and, at Hampton Court Palace: 'a very clear looking-glass, ornamented with columns and little images of alabaster'.[1] The probate inventory of the possessions of the Earl of Leicester, taken at Leicester House in 1588, records that there were in the Wardrobe 'Three great glasses, one standing in a verie faire frame, with beares and ragged staves on the top, with a steele glasse in it, the other ij of cristall', value 40s.[2] This is an instance of a description differentiating clearly between metal and glass; a distinction often left indeterminate.

Almost all Tudor looking-glasses must have been diminutive because, first, steel[3] was limited in size by its weight and the problem of polishing the surface and, secondly, glass again was restricted in area by primitive techniques in both making the material and in silvering it. Today, most of the looking-glasses that existed in the time of Henry VIII and Elizabeth I would be classed as jewellery rather than furniture, and they probably stood on tables or were kept in drawers to be brought out when required for exhibition or use. In many cases they were too highly valued to be left permanently exposed, and too insignificant to be sufficiently decorative hanging on a wall.

It is not until the later seventeenth century that glass became common enough in large sizes for its popularity to be assured as a wall decoration. In fact, by 1667 Sir Samuel Morland, diplomatist and inventor, had installed in his house at Vauxhall a room of which the walls were covered entirely in looking-glass, a somewhat unnerving decorative scheme adopted also by Nell Gwynne and Louise de Keroualle, Duchess of Portsmouth. The latter's mansion was visited in the 1670s by the Moorish ambassador, who commented that he 'much wondered at the room of glass where he saw himself in a hundred places'.

Comparable in rarity and extravagance with glass-lined walls were looking-glasses framed in silver. These were made often *en suite* with a pair of candlestands and a table, usually of wood overlaid, wholly or partly, with the metal decorated with embossed and engraved designs. Three such looking-glasses are in the Royal Collection at Windsor Castle, one of about 1670 with the cypher of Charles II, another of about 1697 with that of William III, and a third entered in an inventory of 1725 as having belonged to the 'Queen Dowager'. This latter might have been either Catherine of Braganza, who had been the Queen of Charles II and died in 1705, or Henrietta Maria, Queen of Charles I who had died in 1669. A suite made of ebony mounted with plaques of silver is at Knole, Kent, and a set of candlestands, looking-glass and table, of walnut and silver, from Penn House, Buckinghamshire, was sold at an auction in London in 1928 for 10,100 guineas. A few others exist and many, with and without looking-glasses, have disappeared with the passing years. One of them received a mention by Celia

---

[1] *Paul Hentzner's Travels in England*, ed. Horace Walpole, 1797, pages 32 and 57.
[2] *Archaeologia*, 73, 1923, page 28.   [3] See page 143.

Fiennes when she was in Derbyshire in 1696: visiting Bretby, a mansion demolished in about 1785 but rebuilt thirty years later, she wrote of seeing one of the bedrooms in the house. 'This best', she recorded, 'was the bride Chamber wch used to be Call'd ye Silver roome where ye stands, table and fire utensills were all massy silver, but when plate was in nomination to pay a tax, ye Earle of Chesterfield sold it all. . . .'

Silver was used also to frame the looking-glasses forming part of the suite of accessories for the dressing-table, a fashion that was introduced some time after 1660 and continued until about the middle of the eighteenth century. Some of these sets comprise more than two dozen pieces, with receptacles for combs, pins, patches, powder—

'The Table Miroir, One Glue Pot,
One for Pomatum, and whatnot?'[1]

These were extreme and fanciful fashions and most citizens in the last part of the seventeenth century, however wealthy they may have been, were content with less ostentation. The average frame, made of decorated wood, was at first often indistinguishable from that used for a painting, and not every surviving example shows distinctively that it was intended for enclosing a looking-glass. Sometimes this is obvious when a frame, otherwise acceptable as having been produced especially for the purpose, is obviously larger than the size of the glass that could have been manufactured at the time and could have been intended only for a picture.

The majority of the frames were of a nearly-square shape and of a simple rounded section: the so-called 'cushion' shape. Each was surmounted by a deep arched top that has often been mislaid or destroyed, and while they conformed to one another in general outline their sizes varied. What they may have lacked in the way of differing design, they made up for with a wide variety of decorative treatments. They were veneered in a number of woods ranging from walnut to the most exotic importations, and either left quite plain to show off the carefully selected graining or inset with marquetry.

Alternatively, the highly fashionable lacquer work, imported from China, was used sometimes, and the rare looking-glass set within a frame of equal rarity. For this purpose use was made of the type of lacquer known at the time as 'Bantam' and today as 'Coromandel', the flat ground incised with patterns which were then coloured and gilded. The Chinese artist completed such work in the form of large-sized panels measuring two feet or so in width and as much as seven or eight feet tall, which were hinged together into four-, six-, eight- or twelve-fold draught-screens, each with a continuous scene on one side or both. Arriving in England, they were taken apart, cut into suitably sized pieces and reused in the form of veneer on frames and other furnishings or, occasionally, to form the panelling of small rooms. The carefully composed traditional Oriental stories were hacked into nonsense, but the material was genuinely lacquer from Far Cathay and that was what mattered at the time.

Frames decorated in the home were also used, although it is not always easy to differentiate between amateur and professional workmanship. Japanning, the Western equivalent to Orien-

[1] John Evelyn, *Mundus Muliebris*, 1690. See Charles Oman, *English Domestic Silver*, fourth edition, 1959.

tal lacquer, was widely popular from the last quarter of the seventeenth century, and John Stalker and George Parker's well-known book, *A Treatise of Japanning and Varnishing*, published in 1688, gave excellent instructions for its performance as well as providing engraved designs to be copied. 'Filigree' or 'Curled Paper' was another type of decorative art practised in the home. The rolls of tinted and gilded paper were formed into complex patterns which are to be admired more for their ingenuity than anything else, and it is to be wondered that even the few surviving examples that have surrounded looking-glasses for a matter of two and a half centuries should have escaped destruction from the hands of time and man.

Needlework was a further branch of domestic art employed occasionally in framing. A well-known frame at Port Sunlight[1] incorporates filigree work which itself frames a number of small panels of stumpwork embroidery surrounding a piece of looking-glass. Others are entirely of stumpwork: that strangely named variety of padded embroidery made during the seventeenth century, which embellished the clothing of its miniature figures with metal threads and sequins and used scraps of shining talc to simulate windows and fishponds. Small brightly coloured glass beads were also used sometimes for the embroidering of frames, and perhaps give the twentieth-century onlooker an idea of the original brilliance of silk-worked examples before light and air dimmed them.

At least one specimen of a seventeenth-century frame decorated with dyed straw has been preserved, and shows typical late Stuart figures and *motifs* worked in the fragile material on a ground of grey silk.[2] This does not exhaust the list of unusual embellishments, but proves that the craftsmen of the time, both amateurs and professionals, spared no pains in devising ingenious settings for the glass.

Although the majority of remaining looking-glasses of the years 1670–85 were in frames of comparatively plain 'cushion' pattern, a number have survived in more elaborate form. These, with a glass also more or less square in shape, are carved heavily with amorini, fruit and flowers and much else, and at one time were (and occasionally still are) attributed invariably to the overworked chisel of Grinling Gibbons. Their overall shape varies little from that of the 'cushion' frame; in rare instances the elaborate cresting centres on a coat of arms that makes close dating possible.

With the increased attention paid to the fireplace from about 1690, a looking-glass was often placed above the mantelshelf. Long and low in shape, it was made from three pieces of glass: two roughly square, of which one was placed at either side of a larger central piece with the joins left unconcealed but bevelled. Some examples have an arched centre glass, others have a serpentine upper edge with all three pieces shaped. Rarely, they remain inset in the panelling of the room for which they were made and of which they form an integral part. At about the same time came the introduction of tall glasses, named pier-glasses after the solid uprights of masonry between windows, which were placed beside the windows of a room. These were a great advance in decoration, for not only did the glasses reflect whoever or whatever stood

[1] Ralph Edwards, *The Shorter Dictionary of English Furniture*, 1965, page 317, fig. 1.
[2] Victoria and Albert Museum, W108—1937.

in the light thrown by the windows, but they brightened and artificially enlarged the apartment.

The pier-glass was composed of an upright rectangular sheet of looking-glass of the largest size that could be afforded by the purchaser, and above this was placed a further piece of glass, smaller and usually with an arched top; alternatively, the larger sheet was replaced by two or more of lesser area. Joins where the sheets met were often masked, and there were various ways of doing this: by means of a narrow strip of bevelled glass, by the cutting of a pattern in the glass that embraced the join and distracted the eye from it, or by the superimpositon of a wood fillet.

Framing of both pier- and chimney-glasses took a number of forms, but, on the whole, woodwork was kept to a minimum and formed only a very unobtrusive proportion of the whole. Borders of coloured glass, cut with plain bevels or more complicated patterns, were used sometimes, or the principal glasses were enclosed within a frame of *verre églomisé* (see page 134), the joins in the glasses forming the border being masked either with narrow pieces of engraved brass or with gilt paper. Crestings were sometimes elaborately carved in wood and gilded, and their design owes much to French inspiration. The contemporaneous looking-glasses of the Louis XIV period are easily confused with English ones, and it is often difficult to decide which side of the Channel saw their origin; a problem that is common to other furniture of the period.

The man whose name is associated with design at the time in England was Daniel Marot (*c.* 1663–1752), a Frenchman who fled his native country for Holland and then London, and after 1685 styled himself 'architect to William III, King of England'. Little is known of his career here beyond the facts that he laid out the gardens of Hampton Court Palace, and published designs for furniture from 1700 onwards (derived from Italian sources) that show he was familiar with the *motifs* fashionable throughout Europe. Probably he studied the work of Jean Bérain, the Parisian who in 1674 was appointed to the post of *dessinateur de la Chambre et du Cabinet du Roi*, whose published engravings, and those of others, doubtless circulated on both sides of the Channel. Marot's work shows frames for looking-glasses of oval and rectangular shapes in simple half-round mouldings ornamented at intervals with scrolls and shells, with heavy crestings in the form of masks, coats of arms, or mythological figures. The flowing exuberance of the original Italian models is greatly restrained, and the comparatively inert results owe much to the sober Dutch taste of Marot and the Court.

While japanning continued to be employed for furniture and frames, its use for the latter diminished as the eighteenth century progressed, and gilding, which gained popularity during the reign of Charles II, became increasingly fashionable from then onwards. In order to form a sufficiently smooth surface for gilding, the roughly-carved woodwork had to be coated with a composition known as gesso. The ingredients of this varied with time, and each user had his personal preferences with which to achieve a desired effect: 'Armenian bole', known now as gilder's red clay, ground in glair (white of egg mixed with water), was recommended by the Paduan, Cennino Cennini, in 1437, and in the eighteenth century candle grease was added sometimes and parchment size substituted for the glair. The gesso was applied thinly in successive coats, each being allowed to dry before the next was added, and each was smoothed carefully until a final surface like polished ivory was obtained. Whereas the basic shaping and carving were carried out in the pinewood of which the frame was usually made, details in low relief were carved into the gesso itself. This was ornamented further, if required, by stamping the flat background parts with a circular metal punch to provide a broken surface, or a granular effect was gained by sprinkling those areas with sand and covering them in the normal way with gesso and gilding.

The next stage in gilding was to tint the gesso surface with a coating of yellow ochre to disguise any areas that might not be covered subsequently with the gold leaf. Then, a part at a time, the work was wetted to make it 'tacky' and the leaf placed on it. When the whole was covered, it could be burnished where required with a dog's tooth or an agate, and it was usual to enhance the high-standing parts in this way and leave the background contrastingly dull. Silver leaf, which was cheaper, was used in a similar way, but it would discolour quickly unless protected by varnish. Sometimes the silvered article was coated with a yellow-stained varnish to make it appear as if gilded.

Occasionally, use was made of the alternative process of oil-gilding, by which the gesso surface was painted with an oil-based size and then covered with gold leaf. The finish was more durable than that obtainable by the water-gilding outlined above, but the surface could not be burnished and the process was appropriate more for outside work than for the interior of the home.

The vogue for gilding and the carved gesso surfaces on which it was employed coincided with a fashion for looking-glasses of a smaller size. They show a wide range of patterns combining the shell details of Daniel Marot with a free use of acanthus and other foliage. Interlacing patterns of *laub und bandelwerk*, found painted on pottery and porcelain of the time, lent themselves very well to reproduction in low relief, and were used frequently on the flat borders surrounding the glass. The finished frames owed much to the men who made them; while the basic patterns came from outside sources, such as engraved designs, the frame-maker and the gilder interpreted them according to their own tastes and gave an English idiom to the foreign designs on which they relied. It is rare for one looking-glass to resemble another very closely, and even one of a pair will reveal some divergence of detail from the other. This, incidentally, applies to most furniture made in the eighteenth century, when hand workmanship was employed exclusively, but it is apparent particularly in the case of gesso-coated pieces on which the relief patterns are markedly individual.

The shape most commonly found shows a glass of upright rectangular form, the frame with narrow sides, the deep top centring on a cartouche or other ornament, and the shallow lower member reminiscent of the upper and repeating the central *motif*. Glasses of this type survive in large numbers, and their appearance and size make them extremely popular for use in modern rooms. Many were fitted at the lower corners with shaped brass plates into which metal candle-arms were placed.

20

The decade 1720–30 saw carved and gilt gesso frames vying in popularity with comparatively plain ones veneered with walnut. These latter relied for their effect on their shaped outlines, with an occasional slight addition of gilding in the form of an inner carved and gilt slip immediately round the glass, and sometimes gilt cresting and apron ornaments. The former was often an eagle with outstretched wings, and both were sometimes in the shape of the popular scallop shell. Looking-glasses of the period, especially the plainer ones of small size, were fashionable once again in the years 1920–30, and large numbers of reproductions of differing quality were put on the market. Most of them reveal themselves at a glance for what they are, but occasional examples need careful examination before their lack of age, and usually merit also, becomes apparent.

The low and wide overmantel-glass also changed in shape and size with the years, and about 1740–50 there was sometimes above the fireplace a very big frame divided into two parts. In the lower part would be a looking-glass, often in three pieces like those of earlier date, and in the upper would be displayed an oil-painting. This arrangement did not do justice to the latter, on the whole, and the fashion endured only fitfully.

By 1730, it was apparent that much of the influence of Marot and his followers had waned and there came a reintroduction of the seventeenth-century correctness of Inigo Jones, who in turn interpreted the rules of the Italian, Andrea Palladio. The lead in this came from Richard Boyle, Earl of Burlington, and his protégé William Kent. While the architectural achievements of these years—Holkham, Badminton and elsewhere—lie outside the scope of this volume, Kent did not limit his work and influence to the exteriors of mansions, but embellished also the apartments within.[1] These, in contrast to the simple and severe frontages, exhibit a large-scale magnificence, with their furnishing seen against walls rising some thirty feet and more to heavily decorated, coffered and painted ceilings. He was the first man in this country to combine the roles of architect and interior decorator, and his work can best, and most fairly, be judged in those mansions where it remains *in situ*.

It was an age in which architecture was taken with great seriousness and studied closely; an age in which a gifted amateur like Lord Burlington could find scope for his talents. On occasions, however, the professionals seem to have fared badly, and Sarah, Duchess of Marlborough typically suggested building a house without their aid. To her grand-daughter, wife of the 4th Duke of Bedford, she wrote in 1732: 'I know of none that are not mad or ridiculous,

---

[1] Horace Walpole wrote of the versatile Kent: 'He was a painter, an architect, and the father of modern gardening. In the first character, he was below mediocrity; in the second, he was a restorer of the science; in the last, an original, and the inventor of an art that realises painting. . . . He was not only consulted for furniture, as frames of pictures, glasses, tables, chairs, &c., but for plate, for a barge, for a cradle. And so impetuous was fashion, that two great ladies prevailed on him to make designs for their birthday gowns. The one he dressed in a petticoat decorated with columns of the five orders; the other like a bronze, in a copper-coloured satin, with ornaments of gold.' H. Walpole: *Anecdotes of Painting* (ed. R. N. Wornum), 3 vols., 1876, vol. III, pages 57 and 58.

Kent died in 1748 at the age of sixty-four, and was buried in Lord Burlington's vault at Chiswick church. For full particulars of his career see Margaret Jourdain: *The Work of William Kent*, 1948.

and I really believe that anybody that has sense with the best workmen of all sorts could make a better house without an architect, than has been built these many years.'[1]

It is, perhaps, little wonder that this general preoccupation should be reflected within the home, and that features seen normally on the exterior should be adapted for the inside. Thus, like the entrance doorways and window framings, the looking-glass frame was often flanked by columns and surmounted invariably by a triangular pediment; the latter broken and centring on a mask, cartouche, or the ubiquitous shell. The depth of the frieze permitted the addition of further ornamental features to contrast with, or to match, those at top and bottom. In some instances, however, the lower member was straight and slight so that the glass could rest on the marble top of a matching pier-table. Decoration at either side of the frame was often present and took the form of pendant swags of fruit, falling drapery or, sometimes, terms to link with a mask in the frieze. Carving was bold, and the finish either gold leaf or paint.

Kent's copyists and followers were numerous. Foremost was John Vardy, his associate in the Office of Works in which Kent was at first Master Mason and from 1737 Deputy Sur-veyor-General. In 1744 Vardy published *Some Designs of Mr Inigo Jones and Mr William Kent*, and included among them were some for overmantel- and pier-glasses. Some of his own origi-nal drawings are preserved in the library of the Royal Institute of British Architects, London, and these include one for a pier-table and looking-glass which has been traced to Hackwood Park, Hampshire.[2]

Another copyist was William Jones, architect of the once-famous Rotunda at Ranelagh; a hall of entertainment now to be seen only in prints or read of in memoirs of the eighteenth century. His publication of 1739, *The Gentlemen's or Builders' Companion*, shows designs for tables and pier-glasses which are severely Palladian in style. Although many surviving ex-amples approximate to them, none has been identified as doing so exactly. The 'architec-tural' type of looking-glass frame achieved a popularity from 1730 until about the middle of the century, but by 1745, when Abraham Swan, a carpenter and joiner, published the first edition of *The British Architect*, he showed designs of Kent's classical type 'overlaid with mis-understood rococo ornament.'[3] He was not alone in attempting the impossible task of blending these opposites, but such faint-hearted essays to be up-to-date were overshadowed speedily by the work of others more sensitive to the revolutionary changes in design that were taking place.

[1] *Letters of a Grandmother*: edited by G. Scott Thomson, 1943, page 52.

[2] See Anthony Coleridge: *John Vardy and the Hackwood Suite*, in *The Connoisseur*, January, 1962 (vol. CXLIX, page 12).

[3] P. Ward-Jackson: *English Furniture Designs of the Eighteenth Century*, 1958, page 36. No. 38, a chimney-piece and overmantel, clearly shows this feature.

2

Rococo

THE asymetrical rococo, known popularly in later years as the 'Chippendale' style, began to make an appearance in England some years after it had been introduced in France. There, two of its leading exponents were Nicholas Pineau and Juste-Aurèle Meissonnier; the latter a Turin-born designer who became *dessinateur du Cabinet du Roi* in succession to Bérain's son (Jean Bérain II), and who published a series of important pattern books. The web of influences that resulted finally in the creation and spread of rococo throughout Europe has been traced by several writers during the past decades.[1] Its presence began to make itself noticed in England shortly after 1730, when the earliest sets of engraved designs were issued in this country; designs especially suited to use by goldsmiths for ornamenting their work.

The numerous refugee craftsmen working in London must have remained in touch with their native land, and French ideas would have been understood and accepted by them readily. These men would have found it less difficult than English silversmiths to put into practical form changes in design which had originated in the minds of their own countrymen. They would have found a ready market for their productions among wealthy travelled Englishmen, then, as ever, infected with a liking for continental fashions. Following the successful application of surface decoration it was a logical step to alter the shapes of the articles themselves so that they conformed more happily to the ornament they bore; to employ the new style not only for silverware but for furnishings and much else.

In 1740, Matthias Lock, a practical carver as well as a designer, published *A New Drawing*

[1] Notably, Fiske Kimball: *The Creation of the Rococo*, Philadelphia, 1943.

Book of Ornaments, Shields, Compartments, Masks, &c., which gave the British public a suggestion of what was to come; but no more than a suggestion, for the engravings show only details and not complete pieces of furniture. Four years later, the same man issued *Six Sconces,*
in which the earlier *motifs* are augmented and blended in a practical manner to take the form of
a half-dozen frames. These engravings mark a logical transition from one style to another: the
severity of line and heaviness of conception of Kent are still faintly apparent, but it can be seen
that the rococo is ousting them and that the designer is not merely another Abraham Swan.
He has studied and learned his French homework, and applied it with cautious common sense.

Lock's drawings and engravings of the 1750s[1] demonstrate his speedy and complete
mastery of the rococo, and their composition is so brilliant that there can be no hesitation in
acknowledging the pre-eminence of their creator. To him is owed the first appearance of most
of the features of fantasy associated with the rococo in England: the angry exotic birds, dogs,
monkeys, squirrels and other animals, *putti,* and Europeans of both sexes self-consciously mas-
querading as Chinese. Equally, he introduced occasional crocketed Gothic arches, but was
unable to resist allying them rather incongruously with C-scrolls, cabochons and delicate
floral sprays.[2] He is to be credited with the introduction of the girandole in its most extrava-
gant form: the carved giltwood representation of a rustic landscape, an Aesop fable, or a
hunting scene, incorporating in its midst a shaped looking-glass flanked by convoluted candle-
holders of gilt metal.

Lock is the first of the eighteenth-century designers of rococo of whom we possess a
reliable record: many of his original drawings are in the Victoria and Albert Museum, London,
and the Metropolitan Museum of Art, New York, but little or nothing is known about the man
himself. His names are not sufficiently unusual to be outstanding or unique, but an entry in
the Apprentice Records of 1724 may refer to him. Under Lock is:

'Math [son of] Math [of] St. Paul's Shadwell join[er] to Ric[hard] Goldsaddle [of]
St. Mart/Fields carv[er].'

A trade-card signed 'M. Lock Fecit', executed for Henry Jouret, a frame-maker and print-
seller of Maiden Lane, may be compared with the one he engraved for himself; which is
lettered simply 'M. Lock Carver In Tottenham Court Road', and dated 1746.[3] The address is
repeated, with the addition of 'near ye Swan', on the title-page of his 1752 *New Book of Ornaments,* but a single plate showing a cartouche, etc., issued in December, 1746, states that it was
published by him 'in Nottingham Court, Castle Street near Long Acre'.[4]

It has been suggested that Lock may have been employed for a period of some years by
Thomas Chippendale, and that he was the inspiration for many of the designs in the *Director.*
Apart from the evidence of a common interpretation of the style, the argument in support
of this is two-fold: there is a gap in Lock's published work between the years 1752 and 1769,

---

[1] Ward-Jackson, *op cit.,* nos. 52 to 69.   [2] Ibid, no. 56.

[3] Reproduced in Heal: *London Furniture Makers, 1660-1840,* 1953, pp. 88 and 93.

[4] Ward-Jackson, *op. cit.,* page 38.

and there is no record whatsoever of what he may have been doing in that period;[1] and some drawings acquired a century ago by the Victoria and Albert Museum from Lock's grandson comprise work not only by Lock himself, but also some original designs for Chippendale's book. On this evidence, slight but not negligible and based on fair reasoning, there would seem to be a case for assuming a Chippendale-Lock relationship of an unspecified nature. It must be stressed that it has not been suggested Lock actually drew any of the designs used in the *Director*, but that he influenced Chippendale in his conception of the style; which could have occurred from a study of Lock's published engravings, and without the two men meeting. However, it is thought that Lock may have been employed in the St Martin's Lane workshops to execute carving, and also to design furniture to order for clients of the firm.

Unfortunately, the picture is further confused. Another collection of drawings, purchased in 1906 by the Victoria and Albert Museum, from a dealer, but of unknown provenance, contains a number of original designs for pieces in the *Director*. In addition, there is a part of a drawing of a bedstead 'clearly by William Ince' and used in his *Household Furniture* (1759–62), another which 'may confidently be ascribed to Johnson'[2] and appears in his *One Hundred and Fifty New Designs* (1761), three contributed by Chippendale to the anonymous *Household Furniture in Genteel Taste for the year 1760*, and Lock's design in ink for the cartouche on the title-page of his *Six Tables* (1746). With this variety of drawings in mind connected in date and subject only, it might be argued that Lock collected such work; that he happened to acquire a quantity of Chippendale's and that there was apparently no personal connection between the two. It would seem that the matter rests for the present, and it must be hoped that some tangible evidence is brought forth in due course.

In addition to issuing engravings under his own name, Matthias Lock was responsible for *A New Book of Ornaments*, published in 1752 and reissued in 1768, in collaboration with Henry Copland. In the latter year the same publisher brought out *A Book of Tables* by Lock, stating on the title-page that it was issued *by R. Sayer at No. 53 Fleet Street where may be had all the Genuine Works of Lock and Copland*. This appears to attribute to the couple greater fame than their output of books justifies, but it is not unlikely that more of their work awaits discovery.[3]

Regrettably, we know even less about Henry Copland than we do about Lock. It would seem that he was little more than a designer, and did not combine his skill with a pencil and graver with the art of using a chisel to put his theory into practice. The earliest record of him discovered so far is a trade-card engraved for Benjamin Rackstrow, a cabinet-maker and

---

[1] Some notes of carving and other costs on a few of his drawings had been thought to have referred to his activities at this time, and to have been prepared for his supposed employer. Recent discovery of some of the actual pieces of furniture and the fact that they were supplied in about 1743, has weakened the argument. The drawings bearing the notes all relate to articles for Hinton House, Somerset, but there is no record surviving of whether Lock himself, or an employer, was paid for them.

[2] Ward-Jackson, *op. cit.*, page 43.

[3] Some of Lock's engravings were reissued in the nineteenth century, but like those of Thomas Johnson (see *post*) under the name of Chippendale.

statuary in Fleet Street. It is signed *H. Copland inv*. *et Sculp 1738*, and shows a fanciful rococo frame, an idea well to the forefront of design at the time it was executed.[1]

Copland published also *A New Book of Ornaments* of his own in 1746, which shows a selection of typical cartouches, framings and *motifs*, but no actual pieces of furniture. It is a very scarce little book, and of the few recorded copies no two are alike. Some bear the imprint on the title-page: *Published . . . by Copland and Bucksher in Gutter Lane Cheapside, London*, while others omit *and Bucksher*; and other copies bear the date *16 Ap: 1746* on each of the nine plates, while in some they are undated and unsigned. Copland engraved also one signed plate in Robert Manwaring's *Chair-Maker's Guide* of 1766,[2] and a bookplate for J. J. Turner which is signed but undated.[3] As he was not shy at appending his name to his engravings it would seem possible that more examples may come to light in time, and enable his worth to be estimated with greater accuracy.

The surviving identified work of Copland is indeed small in quantity and what there is of it compares favourably with that of Lock. Of the two men, Fiske Kimball and Edna Donnell remarked: 'Within their chosen style in England there was no real advance on, or development of, the models given by Lock and Copland, but only a manifold ringing of the changes, with application of the characteristic motive to all articles of furniture.'[4]

In spite of the lack of any details of his career as well as the dearth of his known work, Copland has been allotted a role that might be considered to be out of all proportion to the available facts. As long ago as 1929 Fiske Kimball and Edna Donnell suggested that he had been responsible for the designs for carved work engraved in the *Director*.[5] This theory was advanced in face of the fact that most of them are signed *T. Chippendale inv*. *et delin.*, and that the author wrote in his Preface: 'I frankly confess, that in executing many of the Drawings, my Pencil has but faintly copied out those Images that my Fancy suggested . . .'. Very slight evidence was adduced to support this charge of deceit on the part of the eminent cabinet-maker, and the principal argument was based on a comparison between a drawing of a festoon of flowers in the Metropolitan Museum and one of Copland's engravings in his *New Book of Ornaments*.

This theory of 'Chippendale's ghosts', Lock as inspiration and Copland as draughtsman, has been criticised in recent years. Mr Ralph Edwards doubted it on several scores: that it is

---

[1] Reproduced in Heal: *London Furniture Makers, 1660–1840*, 1953, page 154, and G. Wills: *Decline of the Rococo in England*, in *Country Life*, Vol. CXXV, page 1031 (1959). See p. 156.

[2] This book comprised much material published in the first instance in 1750 and 1760, and Copland's engraving was therefore not necessarily made at the time the book was published. It is reproduced by Ward-Jackson, *op. cit.*, No. 181, and in style is nearer 1750 than 1766. Five other chairs in Manwaring's *Guide* are compared with this signed example, and Ward-Jackson (page 53) states cautiously that they are 'sufficiently similar in manner to justify a tentative attribution to Copland'. However, the same writer's discussion of the engraver's use of the term *Fecit* after his name, both in his book and on the signed Manwaring plate, is complicated by the fact that he used the more common and positive *inv*. *et Sculp* on the Rackstrow trade-card. Whether this has any significance can hardly be decided on present evidence.

[3] In the Metropolitan Museum, New York (Baillie collection), and reproduced by Kimball and Donnell.

[4] Fiske Kimball and Edna Donnell: *The Creators of the Chippendale Style* in *Metropolitan Museum Studies*, Vol. I, pp. 115–54, New York, 1928–9. [5] Ibid., p. 122.

not possible to attribute furniture drawings to a particular artist on stylistic grounds in the same manner as is often possible with other drawings; a comparison of drawings with engravings is not a reliable one on which to base conclusions; no signed drawing by Henry Copland is known. Finally, he is not satisfied 'that Chippendale may not after all have been responsible for a number of the drawings for the *Director*, all of which he signed, and at least that he may be credited with the case pieces'.[1] Elsewhere, and later, the same authority wrote: '. . . in the production of the *Director* designs there was a considerable measure of collaboration, that Lock was associated with Chippendale as a draughtsman, and that Copland was responsible for the great majority of the designs in their *finished* state may be accepted.'[2]

The chain of reasoning by which Lock and Copland have been 'fathered' with much of Chippendale's work is as tenuous as it is ingenious, and may be summarised as follows: Copland collaborated with Lock in a book issued in 1752, and had published one of his own, with the same title incidentally, six years before. Matthias Lock was the foremost designer in the rococo manner. Because he published no books between 1752 and 1769 and there is no record of his activities during those years, which coincided with the period when Chippendale was preparing his *Director* for the press, he may have been in the latter's employ at least between those dates. As this is a possibility, then his one-time collaborator, Henry Copland, may have been concerned in the same enterprise, and his role was either that of originating designs or preparing for the engraver those of Chippendale.[3]

The inclusion of Copland in this chain of reasoning is difficult to justify. On the evidence, to shoulder him with the responsibility of having done most of Chippendale's work for him, if, indeed, such assistance was necessary, is taking it for granted that no one else was capable of the task. By 1754, the year when the *Director* was published, the rococo style was no longer a novelty, and had a 'ghost' been required the choice was not restricted to Copland. Pending the production of more convincing documents, it is only fair to return to Chippendale the credit for the designs he claimed as his own two centuries ago.

Thomas Chippendale's *The Gentleman and Cabinet Maker's Director* was published in 1754. It was an ambitious production both on account of the quantity of engravings, the variety of pieces they depicted and the size of the actual pages: folio, about 18 by 11 inches. The dedication to the Earl of Northumberland is followed by a Preface of the type not uncommon in books of the period, written in a stilted manner and conveying the minimum of meaning in the maximum of words. The 161 plates were engraved by Matthew Darly, J. S. Müller and T. Müller,[4] and among them are designs for looking-glasses depicted with variations to be adopted to suit the taste of a client.

[1] Margaret Jourdain, revised by Ralph Edwards: *Georgian Cabinet-Makers*, 3rd edition 1955, page 22 note.

[2] Thomas Chippendale: *A New Edition of The Gentleman and Cabinet Maker's Director*, introduction by Ralph Edwards, 1957.

[3] Peter Ward-Jackson, *op. cit.*, page 44, points out our complete lack of knowledge of Copland's activities following his collaboration with Lock in 1752. After that, 'for all we know, he may have been dead'.

[4] Johann Sebastian Müller (1715– c. 1785) and his brother Tobias came from Nuremburg in the mid-1750s and settled in London. The former called himself by an anglicised version of his name, John Miller.

The publication of the book was noticed in the *Gentleman's Magazine* of April, 1754 (Vol. XXIV, page 195) in the list of books published, under the headings of MECHANICKS:

'The gentleman's and cabinet-makers director. By *Thomas Chippendale*. 2l. 8s.'

It was advertised also in newspapers, and the *General Evening Post* carried a series of six announcements in consecutive issues beginning with that for 30th May–1st June, stating that the price was 37 shillings unbound. A new parliament met on 31st May and the notices were timed obviously to go into print after the hubbub of the election was over, but when the members would be in London and might perhaps make time to pay a call at the St Martin's Lane workshops. To this end, a postscript ran: 'N.B. All Sorts of Cabinet and Upholstery Work made by the Author in the neatest and most fashionable Taste, and at the most reasonable Rates.'

In 1755 a second edition appeared, but it varies only in minor details from the first. Seven years later, in 1762, Chippendale published a third edition. This was a revision of the earlier ones and contained a total of 200 plates; some of the former ones were replaced and there were a number of additional engravings by various hands. Publication of the *Director* was announced once again in the *Public Advertiser* on 8th March, 1766, but no book followed. From the evidence of three unpublished finished and inked drawings it is thought that the author contemplated but abandoned a fourth and further-revised edition.

The number of looking-glasses in the 1754 edition altered in design and increased in quantity by 1762. Their patterns were far more advanced in the rococo manner than the earlier ones; the cautious lines of the latter were replaced by the more masterly exuberances that later so shocked his detractors and were a source of satisfaction to his admirers. They show no signs of the Neo-classicism which was then so imminent, but Chippendale was so strongly steeped in the style with which his name was inescapably linked that a change at that juncture might have disturbed his clientèle and ruined his business.

The rococo of Thomas Chippendale coincided with the height of the mid-century vogue for Chinoiserie, and in many instances it is difficult to determine the French from the Chinese, or pseudo-Chinese, in his work; the two were intermingled with such success that 'Chinese Chippendale' is almost a style in its own right. What is clearer is his use of Gothic; the straight or arched line in contradistinction to the sweeping curves imported from across the Channel. More than any other well-known designer of the period, Chippendale was affected by the fashion for this very English style: a style esteemed and exploited by a select circle of whom Horace Walpole was the energetic centre. Apart from Walpole and his friends, Gothic was not popular except in small doses, and its occasional adoption in concentrated form was, and is, perhaps, considered more eccentric than attractive.

Its use was championed on both artistic and patriotic grounds. Its respectable origins and use in the building of churches made it acceptable as a truly English style in preference to anything the Continent offered, for we were at war with the French, on and off, for most of the eighteenth century and purists argued that the art of the enemy was no less abhorrent than the enemy himself. On the other hand, it was debated whether a style used traditionally for ecclesiastical purposes was not out of place in a secular building. The employment of Gothic *motifs* on looking-glass frames was often in uneasy conjunction with C-scrolls and even with a suggestion of Chinoiserie, the latter seeming seldom to be submerged completely, but was far from common and rarely was the result entirely a happy one. While it might contribute to the monastic 'gloomth' of Strawberry Hill, it was seldom chosen as the background against which to raise a family.

Allied in manner and mannerisms to much of the work in the later *Director* was that of the carver and designer Thomas Johnson. His *Twelve Gerandoles* of 1755 was followed by a book, issued first in parts and without a title, that appeared in due course as *One Hundred and Fifty New Designs* (1761).[1] Others of his engravings had a chequered career terminating in the nineteenth century with their publication minus his name and with that of Chippendale substituted. Only one drawing definitely by him and another attributed to him are known, and as little is recorded about his life as about the lives of most of his fellow craftsmen.[2] He was baptised on 13th January, 1714, at St. Giles-in-the-Fields, but the dates and places of his birth and death remain undiscovered; nor do we know the occupation of his father, also named Thomas, or where the son received his training.

He was declared bankrupt in September, 1764, and the announcement in the *London Gazette* noticed him as 'Thomas Johnson, of Store-street, in the Parish of Saint Giles in the Fields in the County of Middlesex, Carver and Painter'.[3] His workshop was situated in Tottenham Court Road at the corner of Store Street, and the use of the latter as his address may have been a device to lessen publicity over these proceedings. At any rate, no trace of them, except for brief notices in print, appear to have survived. The fact that he was termed both carver and painter is worthy of comment, because some of his identified work is decorated with painting: e.g., the Dunkeld House looking-glass was invoiced as 'white and gold'. Regilding has doubtless befallen many other frames, whose present appearance is thus very different from that when they left their makers' hands.

Johnson employed much the same repertoire as Lock and Chippendale, and no one feature would seem to have been peculiar to any of them. Just as it seems to be apparent that, for instance, Lock favoured the inclusion of an overturned jar spilling water, so this is seen to have been used also by Johnson, and finally the search for such significant details is found to be a futile one. Undoubtedly, each varied from the other in the larger view, Johnson excelling his

[1] When advertising the first part of *One Hundred and Fifty New Designs*, Robert Sayer, the publisher, announced that he had for sale *Twelve Girondoles* (*sic*) at 1s. 6d., which had been sold by the author for 2s. when first issued in 1755, and *A New Book of Ornaments* (1760) at 1s. He offered also copies of Copeland's (*sic*) *Book of Ornaments* (?that of 1746), and *Ornaments for Looking-glass Frames, Chimney-Pieces, &c.*, by M. Lock, at 2s. (*General Evening Post*, 24–27 October, 1761). Ward-Jackson notes reprints of the above published by Sayer in 1768. The latter must either have bought up the remaining stocks of these works from their authors, or purchased the plates and reprinted them at an earlier date than has been assumed hitherto.

[2] Johnson's career and reproductions of his engravings are in H. Hayward: *Thomas Johnson and English Rococo*, 1964.

[3] *London Gazette*, 11–15 September, 1764 (No. 10452).

rivals by the sheer complexity and fluidity of his patterns. This is not so obvious in his engravings, which are encumbered often with feathery branches and flourishes that confuse the main subject, but in such work as has been accepted as being by his hand, or inspired by him, is seen clearly a mastery of the craft of carver that is equalled by very few of his contemporaries.

Increasing attention has been paid to Johnson during the past few years, and amends are being made for the almost complete neglect he had suffered for nearly two centuries. The principal reason for this was undoubtedly because his name was eclipsed by that of Chippendale, whose monumental *Director*, coupled with extensive workshops, contrasted with the other's comparatively slender output. Further, in view of the fact that no bills of Johnson's have come to light and pieces carved by him appear to feature on the accounts of others, it is probable that he worked only as a sub-contractor for more prominent traders.[1] If so, then it is possible he was completely unknown to the general public and to the wealthy patrons who paid him only indirectly.

A feature of the designs of Thomas Johnson and many of his contemporaries is the inspiration they derived from *Aesop's Fables*, of which illustrated editions had appeared in England from 1651 onwards. This first one was the work of John Ogilby, later to achieve a certain notoriety for his prolific output when Dryden ridiculed him in *MacFlecknoe* and Pope in the *Dunciad*, which was followed in 1666 by that of Francis Barlow. His work, for which most of the original drawings are in the British Museum, was reprinted together with an additional 31 plates illustrating the life of Aesop in 1687 and 1703, and made a final appearance with an Amsterdam imprint in 1714.

Matthias Lock copied directly some of the animals and birds depicted by Barlow, and Johnson did likewise. Not only did the Chelsea porcelain factory model a figure of Aesop from the frontispiece of the 1687 and later editions, but the illustrations to the *Fables* themselves were used as models for the painted decoration on tea-sets and other pieces from the early 1750s onwards. At Worcester, in the 1760s, the *Fables* were again in frequent use, and the much-lauded Jeffryes Hamett O'Neale was responsible for many pieces painted with subjects from them in his individual amateurish manner.[2]

None of these men, carvers or painters, had need to rely entirely on early editions of Barlow, for at least two sets of copies of his engravings were published at about the mid-century. Of these, one was the work of James Kirk, who was responsible also for a few of the plates in Johnson's *One Hundred and Fifty New Designs*. The latter volume features a noticeable number of pieces incorporating details taken clearly from Barlow's work,[3] although it is not inferred that Kirk was responsible for this and his dual role is probably only a coincidence.

The last men of importance to be considered as designers of rococo frames are William Ince and Robert Mayhew, who were in partnership as cabinet-makers and together published a book entitled *The Universal System of Household Furniture*. This appeared first in monthly

[1] See George Cole, page 150 and plate 78.
[2] See H. Rissik Marshall: *Coloured Worcester Porcelain*, 1954, chapter 4 and illustrations.
[3] H. Hayward: *op. cit.*, pages 11 and 12, footnotes 24 and 25.

parts beginning in July, 1759, and Mr Ralph Edwards has pointed out that 'the work was obviously intended to rival Chippendale's *Director*, of which the third edition was also appearing serially during the same period'.[1] Later, the plates were issued as a single folio volume with an imposing but undated title-page, and it is assumed that it made its appearance in 1762.

The book shows only a few designs for frames, and these few, like those of most other designers of the time, introduce little or nothing new into the current selection of *motifs*; the C-scrolls, pierced shellwork, garlands, Chinamen and exotic birds are all present, but perhaps in a more restrained manner than with Lock, Johnson and Chippendale. There is, on the whole, little by which to differentiate an Ince and Mayhew frame from one made to the pattern of any other designer of the time,[2] but they are able to hold their own with the best. The pair in the Metropolitan Museum, New York (plate 97), which follows exactly a plate in the *Universal System*, and was perhaps supplied in the first instance by the firm, proves this to be the case. It is not known whether Ince and Mayhew actually made frames on their own premises, or whether they followed what would seem to have been the practice of some others by employing an outside specialist carver for such work as was wanted.

Finally, among the few others recorded as designers mention should be made of Matthew Darly, who embraced the occupations of engraver, designer, caricaturist and publisher between the years 1750 and 1778. As far as looking-glasses are concerned, he issued in collaboration with an otherwise unknown partner named Edwards *A New Book of Chinese Designs* in 1754, and an alternative claim to interest is that he was employed as engraver of many of the plates in the *Director* as well as of all those in Ince and Mayhew's book. Also, a number of trade-cards reproduced by Sir Ambrose Heal[3] bear his signature, and confirm that a rather overwrought Chinoiserie was his recognisable trait.

In each instance, except that of Thomas Chippendale, our present-day knowledge of mid-eighteenth-century designers stems almost exclusively from such of their drawings and engravings as have been preserved fortuitously. We are able to estimate the work of Lock more accurately because so much of his graphic output, although probably no more than a mere fraction of the whole, is in museums in London and New York. There must have been many artists and craftsmen in addition to those discussed above of whose lives and work no traces remain. We are ignorant of the creators of many fine frames or, at best, can ascribe them only on a minimum of debatable evidence. It is to be hoped that future research will enable this position to be corrected.

[1] *The Universal System*, a complete reprint with a preface by Ralph Edwards, 1960, page e.

[2] Evidence of this interdependence is seen in John Mayhew's own copy of Batty Langley's *The City and Country Builder's and Workman's Treasury of Designs* (1740), in the Metropolitan Museum, New York. Interleaved in it are five plates of Matthias Lock's designs.

[3] *Op. cit.*

3
Neo-classical to Regency

THE reaction to rococo in England may be said to have begun in 1758 when the young Edinburgh architect, Robert Adam, returned from his Grand Tour; a tour which had included a lengthy stay in Italy and an expedition to examine and record the ruins of the Emperor Diocletian's palace at Spalato. There has been much argument during the past few decades as to whether the furniture designs of the brilliant Scot were influenced by the Neo-classicists in Paris or whether, in this instance, the trend was reversed and Paris was led by London.[1] Adam visited France, as far as is known, only once and that was when he was on his way to the Mediterranean in 1754; too early for him to have seen any signs of the style to come —if signs were there. While it may remain debatable whether he originated the design of Neo-classical furniture, there can be no question of his having been in the forefront of its exponents. While he was in Rome he was able to become acquainted with many of the leaders of the *avant-garde* movement of the time; among them Piranesi and Winckelmann. In such a circle, a young man of keen artistic perception could hardly have failed to become imbued with a desire to put new ideas into practice. Not only did Robert Adam prove to have the ability to do this successfully, but on returning to England he was fortunate in attracting patrons who gave him the opportunities.

During the second quarter of the eighteenth century William Kent had made use of

[1] The controversy was started by Fiske Kimball in two articles in the *Gazette des Beaux Arts: Les Influences anglais dans la formation du style Louis XVI* (1931, pp. 29–44 and 231–5), and has been dealt with by E. Harris: *The Furniture of Robert Adam*, 1963.

ancient Roman decorative themes preserved in the catacombs of Rome which had been adapted in the early sixteenth century by Raphael and Giovanni da Udine for the adornment of the Villa Madama. Against the proportions of Kent's rooms with their early- and mid-Georgian mouldings, the effect of the delicate grotesques was slight and their popularity limited. Adam made a careful study of the originals and some of his drawings of the Villa Madama are in the Soane Museum, London; in addition, he was able to take advantage of the newly-publicised discoveries at Herculaneum and Pompeii. He condemned the earlier architect's use of such *motifs* in conjunction with disproportionate surroundings, and replaced them with his own carefully considered versions of the Classical. The heavy swags of flowers and fruit, the massive shells and masks, and the deeply moulded pediments on frames were replaced by the slightest of ornaments: the narrowest of graceful chains of husks or *Garrya Elliptica* catkins, rows of anthemion (honeysuckle), round and oval paterae, and sphinxes seated among leafy scrolls centring on carefully proportioned urns flanked by griffins and held aloft on columns in the form of female terms.

At its most refined and dainty it is perhaps not surprising that the arch Gothicist, Horace Walpole, sneeringly wrote of 'Mr Adam's gingerbread and sippets of embroidery'.[1] George III said much the same when admitting to Benjamin West that he was a traditionalist. West reported the conversation to his friend Joseph Farington, who duly noted it in his Diary in the form of the King's actual words: 'I am a little of an Architect and think that the Old School (that of Lord Burlingtons period which had more of magnificence) is not enough attended to, —that the Adam's have introduced too much of neatness & prettiness . . .'[2] Both comments were made, however, when the style had been current for many years, had become cheapened by widespread imitation, and there was reason for many less exalted and unprejudiced persons to have become wearied of it.

It has been pointed out recently that although Robert Adam designed furniture, the quantity is much less than has been supposed.[3] His work in that field most frequently took the form of what may be termed 'fixtures': console and side tables, fittings for bows and niches, and looking-glass frames for placing over tables or chimney-pieces. The use of a simple curved line, not serpentine as formerly, is pronounced, and is to be seen not only in the shaping of table-tops but in the central glass of a three-plate overmantel which often was given a semi-circular top. In many examples this was covered in a filigree pattern too delicate to be carved in wood, and therefore made from composition moulded on wires or from metal. Columnar supports at the sides followed the pattern of those he used for chairs and tables: soberly straight and tapered, with none of the exuberantly swirling curves of the mid-century.

The imitators of Adam seized on the most popular elements of his work and reproduced them continually, with the result that the resource of their originator tends sometimes to be overlooked. Like those of his fellow-designer, William Kent, his frames and other furnishings

---

[1] Letter to the Countess of Upper Ossory, 17th September, 1785. Toynbee ed., vol. XIII, p. 321.
[2] On 16th January, 1800. *The Farington Diary*, ed. J. Greig (1923), vol. I, page 284.
[3] E. Harris, *op. cit.*

look their best in the surroundings for which they were especially intended. Neither man was a furniture designer in the sense of planning articles for general manufacture in the manner of Chippendale, Ince or Sheraton, and each of their pieces was intended for a specific position in a studied scheme of decoration. Like so many innovators Robert Adam has suffered from having had his true reputation confused by the work of his many followers.

One of the best-known exponents of Adam's designs was the London carver and cabinet-maker, John Linnell, whose premises were in Berkeley Square in the west end of London. More is known about his work than about that of many of his contemporaries because a considerable number of his drawings have been preserved and are in the Victoria and Albert Museum. He supplied furniture for many important clients, and some of his pieces have been identified from his drawings or from descriptions in surviving bills.

Linnell's designs for looking-glass frames embrace the close of the rococo style as well as the Neo-classical. His essays in the former are comparatively restrained, with an absence of violent asymmetry and few signs of the Chinoiserie that distinguishes much of the work of Chippendale and his school. His style is midway between the two, and he seems to have indulged in the excesses of neither. He favoured oval-shaped glasses, but no more than did his contemporaries, and would seem to have had a fondness for surmounting many of his frames with a finial in the form of a basket of flowers. It cannot be said, however, that this was peculiar to Linnell and, on the whole, his frames have little by which to identify them and many must remain undiscovered until more of his drawings are published.

Other designers found it no difficult matter to turn from the old to the new, and both Matthias Lock and Matthew Darly made drawings and published engravings of their versions of the Neo-classical. Lock, in particular, must have felt the limitations of the style; one which was composed of a number of set elements that could be varied only in their arrangement, and left little scope for self-expression. Thus, the majority of frames in the Adam manner are very often charming in themselves, but the basis of their design, the formality of the style, only rarely permitted the emergence of the designer's personality. This may have been because Robert Adam himself was so outstanding that no other man approached his mastery. Certainly, his work is far and away above that of his contemporaries, and even when cruelly divorced from the surroundings for which it was so carefully designed it retains clear signs of his individuality.

A feature of many rooms towards the end of the eighteenth century and onwards was the framed convex looking-glass, which came into prominence when it was found possible to make the glasses cheaply and in quantity. This type of reflector has a long ancestry, and examples are depicted in illuminated manuscripts and early oil-paintings. One of the best known of all is in the National Gallery, London: the full-length portrait of Giovanni Arnolfini and Giovanna Cenami painted in 1434 by Jan van Eyck. The couple are shown standing inside a house with a framed circular convex glass on the wall behind them; in it can be seen reflected in miniature the backs of the sitters, other persons, and the remainder of the room.[1]

[1] An interesting mid-eighteenth-century reference to the use of such glasses as an aid to painting pictures was made by the French artist and writer, Jean-Baptiste Descamps. (J.-B. Descamps: *La vie des peintres Flamands, Alle-*

It is known that they were made at Nuremburg in Germany during the fifteenth century, and continued to be manufactured in small numbers from that time onwards. In France in the eighteenth century there is evidence of a larger output, but very little research has been done on the subject. The *Annonces, affiches, et avis divers* of 4th February, 1765, announced:

'*La manufacture des miroirs concaves et des glaces courbées, établie par arrêt du Conseil du 8 Septembre, 1756, devient de plus en plus utile.*'

Silvered glass of all sizes was supplied, also '*loupes à eau, composées de deux glaces concaves remplies d'eau distillée*', and orders were taken at the office in the *rue des Prouvaires, la première porte cochère à gauche par la rue Saint-Honoré* or could be sent direct to *M. Bernière, contrôleur général des ponts et chaussées*, owner of the manufactory.[1]

There is no proof that such glasses were not made before this date in France, and it may be supposed that convexes from the factory above, and others, were imported into England along with flat sheets of looking-glass. Some examples of framed convex glasses datable to about 1760 have been preserved, but they are very few in number and it would seem doubtful whether they were popular at that date. Ince and Mayhew, principally remembered as cabinet-makers and designers of furnishings, were importers of plate glass and presumably also of convexes, and it is interesting to notice that they were the first to print patterns for framing such glasses. Their *Universal System* (1759–62) includes a plate engraved with 'Eight Designs of Frames for Convex or Concave Glasses, which have a very pretty Effect in a well furnish'd Room'. They ring the changes on all the current *motifs*, with 'C'-scrolls, intertwined ribands, rococo leafage and flowers, sprays of leaves, and even a female mask beneath a basket of flowers and with a shell below. The incorporation of a convex glass in the design of a flat plate looking-glass is unusual, but examples are known (plate 84).

By about 1795, stimulated doubtless by the cutting-off of supplies from France due to the Revolution, manufacture of convex glasses was achieved with success at the Ravenhead works of the British Cast Plate Glass Manufacturers.[2] The familiar frame had by then been evolved:

mandes et Hollandais, 4 vols., Paris, 1753–63.) He wrote of the practice of Gerrit Dou (1613–75), whose highly-finished works have certainly a mirror-like quality that may not be just a coincidence:

'It is possible that it is to him that we must attribute an invention—to some extent ingenious but fraught with certain drawbacks—which reduces large objects to a small scale. Dou used a kind of screen fixed to his foot; in the screen he had inserted and framed a concave glass at the height of his eye when he was seated at his easel. This screen formed a species of partition between the object to be represented and the artist. The object was seen in a reduced scale in the concave glass and the artist had only to copy its form and colour.... Dou then drew the objects on to his canvas which was divided into equal squares corresponding to threads on a little frame of the exact size of the circumference of the concave glass, in such a way that when the frame was attached to the glass it represented a square drawn within a circle.'

The above translation by R. H. Wilenski was followed by him with the suggestion that the use of looking-glasses of one type or another was not confined to Dou, but that Vermeer, Fabritius, Hoogstraten and other artists employed them also. (R. H. Wilenski: *An Introduction to Dutch Art*, 1929, pages 280–90.)

[1] Havard: *Dictionnaire de l'Ameblement et de la Décoration*, 4 vols. Paris, 1887–90, vol. II, page 997.

[2] T. C. Barker and J. R. Harris: *A Merseyside Town in the Industrial Revolution, St Helens, 1750–1900*, Liverpool, 1954, page 116. The Minutes of the company record that two cases of convexes and silvered plate were shipped to

the gilt cavetto moulding studded with gilt balls, the inner reeded and ebonised slip, and the whole surmounted by an eagle 'displayed' with a gilt ball suspended from its beak on a chain and with a group of formal foliage at the base of the frame to balance the bird above. Many examples were fitted with a pair of curved arms terminating in candle-holders fringed with cut-glass drops.

More important convex glasses were surmounted by the coat of arms of the original owner, and others were fitted with candle-arms of complex pattern. In this category may be included one for which there is a design in George Smith's *Collection of Designs for Household Furniture* (1808), which has a pair of oil-lamps of classical type suspended from the arms. Another, in the same volume,[1] has an elaborately scrolled top centring on an anthemion, with the upper scrolls utilised as hooks for the suspension chain; this is not only an ugly feature, but would ensure the upper part having to be made of metal to withstand the strain of supporting the whole. Metal was used generally, however, for the candle-arms of such frames, which were gilded and embellished with moulded composition ornament.

Thomas Sheraton wrote of the convex in his *Cabinet Dictionary* of 1803.[2] Under the heading of MIRROR he pointed out that this was 'generally applied to a particular glass, either of convex, or concave surface', and added:

'As an article of furnishing, a mirror is a circular convex glass in a gilt frame, now become universally in fashion, and are considered both as a useful and ornamental piece of furniture.'

The same writer's designs include one for a large sideboard with projecting circular cupboards at either end, each topped by a two-tier dumb-waiter and the brass rails at the back of the middle section centring on a convex mirror. This, like each of the two dumb-waiters, is surmounted by a two-light candelabrum, and the whole is supported on lion mask and paw feet.[3] As engraved, it looks a clumsy and unattractive piece of furniture that shows its designer in one of his frequent moods of inventiveness; moods in which novelty leaves little place for beauty.

The other typical looking-glass of the period 1795–1820 is the overmantel. It took two popular forms: the larger with three plates covering the width of the chimney-piece and with a frieze of classical design above them; and the smaller type, upright, and surmounted either by a

Halifax, Nova Scotia, in March 1815. Four years later it was agreed to advertise in the provincial press the products of the firm, and one of the items noted was convex mirrors ranging from one to three feet in diameter. No mentions of the actual manufacturing process seem to have survived, but 'without much doubt I think the method would have been by pouring the molten glass into cast iron or stone moulds'. (Information from Mr A. E. Owens, Archivist, Pilkington Brothers, Ltd., St. Helens.) Earlier, the author of *The Plate Glass Book* (1757) wrote: 'The Rough Plates are bent at the Glass-House, and then ground, polished and silvered, but have not their *Concavity* or *Convexity* sunk or raised in the grinding or polishing, as is commonly imagined.' Subsequent to writing the above lines, the author has found a Ravenhead price list dated April, 1799. It announces convex and concave mirrors ranging in diameter from 12 to 36 inches, at £2 to £36. 15s. apiece.

[1] Plates 135 and 136. Reproduced in John Harris: *Regency Furniture Designs, 1803–26*, 1961 (Nos. 179 and 180).
[2] Page 271.
[3] T. Sheraton: *Cabinet-Maker, Upholsterer and General Artist's Encyclopaedia*, 1804–8, plate 33.

panel of clear glass decorated with a transferred engraving coloured at the back or with a panel of *verre églomisé*.[1]

Led by the Prince of Wales, whose Saloon at the Pavilion, Brighton, boasted a pier-glass measuring thirteen feet in height by eight feet in width,[2] the wealthy vied with one another in installing glasses of comparable proportions. The frame, in these instances, was of minor importance, and George Smith,[3] suggested the frieze should be dispensed with and the glass 'carried quite to the cornice of the room'.

The lining of the walls of a room with looking-glass, a luxury indulged in by Louis XIV of France at Versailles and imitated across the Channel by those who could afford the tastes of *Le roi soleil*, was revived in at least one apartment in the early nineteenth century. The Colosseum in Regent's Park, London, included a Hall of Mirrors, opened in July, 1835, which had 'at each end . . . three splendid mirrors reaching from the floor to the cornice'. The folding window-shutters were covered also in looking-glass which was revealed when they were closed at night and the cut-glass chandeliers lighted.

A contemporary description of the scene in the Hall evokes much of the magic that was, and still is, inseparable from the looking-glass, and provides a fitting close to this chapter:

'Nothing can exceed the brilliant splendour of the hall when lighted up for the admission of the public; the endless reduplications of reflection from the mirrors give it an appearance of interminable extent in every direction; and the various coloured dresses of the company, which assumes the appearance of a countless multitude in constant motion, produce an impression of grandeur, magnificence, and beauty which cannot be adequately described. The whole scene is one effulgent blaze of splendour, perpetually changing as the spectator varies his position, and presenting new combinations of elegance and beauty in endless succession, exceeding the most florid descriptions of oriental magnificence, and realising the most brilliant romances of fairy enchantment.'[4]

[1] See Appendix 2, page 134..

[2] E. W. Brayley: *Illustrations of His Majesty's Palace at Brighton*, 1838, p. 10.

[3] *Op. cit.*, page 22.

[4] W. E. Trotter: *Select Illustrated Topography of Thirty Miles Round London*, 1839. The initials G. H. are appended to the above paragraph.

PART TWO

Glass

*A Brief History of Plate-glass
Manufacture in England*

*The Composition and Manu-
facture of Looking-glass plates*

*Grinding, Polishing, Diamond-
ing and Foiling of Plates*

I

A Brief History of Plate-glass Manufacture in England

In the Middle Ages it was known that glass backed with metal would make a looking-glass, but the materials then available were so impure and the manufacturing methods so clumsy that successful results could have been obtained only rarely. Instead, mirrors made from small-sized plates of polished metal, protected in some instances by a piece of clear glass, were used. Most popular of all was an alloy named Speculum or steel, composed principally of copper and tin. This took and retained a high polish, but was impracticable in sizes larger than about a foot square because it had to be cast in thick and heavy pieces to produce an undistorted surface.[1] Confusingly, it is often difficult to determine whether the word 'glass' in old documents refers to steel or Speculum, to actual glass or even to rock-crystal.

By the middle of the sixteenth century the long-established and energetic Venetian glass industry included a separate branch of looking-glass-makers, whose products were known and envied throughout Europe. This distinction was shared by the other products made on the island of Murano, where the glasshouses were concentrated to avoid the hazards of fire, which for long enjoyed a virtual monopoly of glassware of all kinds except the most simple. Although the Venetian workers were restricted in their movements, so that the secrets of the craft should not be learned elsewhere, and it was forbidden to export glass-making tools or broken glass

[1] See page 143.

41

which might be remelted, some of the men were induced to emigrate to other countries and set up rival factories in them.

As far as England was concerned a native industry had been carried on since the departure of the Romans, and by the thirteenth century glass-makers from Normandy, across the Channel, were building and operating small furnaces in the well-wooded parts of Surrey, Sussex and elsewhere, taking advantage of the essential ample supplies of wood fuel to hand. Both clear and coloured window glass was made by these men, but there is no record of their having attempted anything as ambitious as sheet glass suitable for giving reflections. A further group of French immigrants, this time from Lorraine, came in the sixteenth century, but their productions did not differ greatly from those of the Normans.

Following successive attempts to establish glasshouses in London by absconding Venetian craftsmen, who were encouraged by Queen Elizabeth I, Jacopo Verzelini opened a works in Broad Street, in the City of London, where between 1575 and 1592 he produced glasses 'as good cheape or rather better cheape than the drynkyng glasses comonlye broughte from the Cittie of Murano, and other partes of beyond the seas'. There is no mention of home-produced looking-glass at this time, and doubtless the amount required was imported. Its cost would have been so high as to limit demand to the wealthiest, and its importance as an article of decoration was not yet deemed great enough for anyone to attempt rivalling the Venetians in its manufacture.

After the death of Verzelini in 1592 the glass-making industry came under the control of a series of monopolists, who were granted patents giving them the sole rights of manufacture. Each was concerned with the anxiety of the Government over the continual and rapid destruction of woodland, caused no less by the activities of iron-smelters than by those of glass-makers. In 1615 a royal proclamation prohibited the use of wood fuel by the latter, and thenceforward coal was used for firing the furnaces. In the same year a fresh group of men took over the monopoly, and by 1618 one of them, Sir Robert Mansell, a retired admiral, had gained complete possession for himself by buying out his partners.

It is recorded that in March, 1620, the Venetian Ambassador, Girolamo Lando, wrote from London to the Doge and Senate mentioning that the English Government had banned the importation of all glass, and 'by this order they also mean to prohibit looking glasses, of which they make a quantity here'. He continued: 'Various subjects of your Serenity, some outlaws who have taken refuge in this kingdom, where many natives of Murano may now be met, work at making looking-glasses and flint glass or teach how to make them.'[1] Within a year Mansell presented a petition to Parliament stating that he was the first to manufacture looking-glass in this country, and this was because he had had his employees instructed in the necessary techniques. It is known that Sir Robert had business connections with Murano, and there is

---

[1] *Calendar of State Papers (Venice, &c)*, vol. XVI, No. 301. Men of other nationalities were in London also, and doubtless employed at their trade. Nicholas Closson of Amsterdam and Jacob van Leisnelt of Antwerp, looking-glass makers, were noted in *Certificate of Strangers . . . taken 6 Sept. 1618*, edited by W. D. Cooper, 1862. Quoted by W. A. Thorpe: *English Glass*, 3rd edition 1961, page 117 footnote.

no doubt that one or more Venetians were concerned with his enterprise. The relevant portion of the petition reads:

'And as concerning Looking glasses Sir Robert Mansell hathe brought to such perfection, That he hathe Chused our Natives to be so fully instructed and taught therein, That the said glasses are now here made wch was never wont to be in England beforetyme, So that thereby we hope in tyme to sett many hundreds on work wch many as those doo import have never done here, but beyond the Seas.'[1]

Two years later, in 1623, he was granted a renewed patent giving him the sole right to make 'all manner of drinking glasses, broad glasses, window glasses, looking glasses, and all other kind of glasses, bugles, bottles, vials or vessels whatsoever'.

The range of permitted productions was wide, but unfortunately evidence of its actual existence, other than by the written word, has vanished; we have no knowledge of how much of each type of glass was produced or what the great majority of it may have looked like. The inherent fragility of the material in conjunction with its possibly inferior quality have ensured that none of Mansell's looking-glass has survived. Most of our knowledge of it, and of other early glass, is to be gleaned too often only from the descriptions of men who were obviously biased in attempts to further their own interests. Exaggeration is seen to have been an occupational disease of glass-making as much as of other commercial undertakings, and it is often difficult, if not well-nigh impossible, to discern the element of truth in an uncorroborated statement made two centuries and a half, or more, ago.

At an early stage in its development the English glass-making industry suffered the disability of a Duty. On 24th November, 1645, Oliver Cromwell 'ordered that an Excize of Twelve pence shall be laid upon every Twenty Shillings value of Glasse and Glasses of all sorts made within the Kingdom, to be paid by the Maker'.[2] Regarding this impost W. A. Thorpe has written, 'that he should have noticed the glassmakers at all was in itself a compliment to the rising industry, and the quota demanded was so small that no umbrage was taken'.[3] This is a bold assumption if meant seriously; for there can be little doubt that the Duty, although one of only 5 per cent, was resented no less than those which followed in the next two hundred years.

After the restoration of the Monarchy, the Worshipful Company of Glass-sellers and Looking-glass Makers was incorporated and in the same year, 1664, importation was prohibited of: 'Rough Glass-Plates, or Plates wrought into Looking-glass, Spectacles, Burning-glasses, Tubes, or other Wrought Glass-plates.'[4] The armorial bearings of the Company are *Azure a Venetian*

[1] British Museum. Ms. Add. 12496.f. 165.

[2] F. Buckley: *The Taxation of English Glass in the Seventeenth Century*, privately printed, 1914.

[3] *A History of English and Irish Glass*, 2 vols., 1929. Vol. I, page 155.

[4] Importation was allowed against payment of Duty within a few years. By 1668 John Greene and Michael Measey, glass dealers in London, were ordering looking-glass plates in quantity from Venice, adding 'lett all bee unfoil'd'. Their later letters contain instruction to supply two invoices with each consignment; one with the correct cost and another at a lower charge to save Duty. In addition, it was suggested that efforts should be made to conceal some of the items, 'that ye Boxes of Lookeing glasses may not bee soe soone felt by our searchers hear...'. A. Hartshorne: *Old English Glasses*, 1897, pages 440-49.

glass cup between a laverpot of white ware on the dexter and a looking-glass on the sinister all proper.
The Charter granted by Charles II allowed them control of the 'art, trade or mystery of grinding, polishing, casing, foyling and finishing of looking-glasses and in selling glasses and looking-glasses'. The Company was responsible also for the sale of stoneware, hence the 'laverpot of white ware', and in 1676 they agreed with the Fulham potter, John Dwight, 'to buy only of his English manufacture and refuse the foreign'.[1]

Just prior to the date of the incorporation of the Glass-sellers, George Villiers, second Duke of Buckingham, came on the scene. His chequered career is too complex, and mainly irrelevant, to be detailed here, but although his interests are said to have included chemistry, in which Gilbert Burnet wrote 'he thought he was very near the finding of the philosopher's stone', it has been doubted whether his connection with glass was for other than financial reasons. This doubt is not unwarranted in view of the fact that Buckingham was occupied constantly in the thick of political and amorous intrigues with intervals spent cooling his heels in the Tower.[2] As a Gentleman of the Bedchamber to Charles II and a Privy Councillor he must have experienced less difficulty than many in obtaining a patent to make glass, which he extended slowly into a near-monopoly. It is known that the Duke had control of a number of patents held in the names of others. One of them, granted in 1662 to Thomas Tilson relating to the making of 'christall glass and looking glass plates', was excepted especially from the jurisdiction of the Glass-sellers' Company and the subject of a clause to this effect in their Charter.

One of the Duke's glasshouses was at Vauxhall, where mirror-glass was made and the manager, John Bellingham, had sold to his employer secrets of the manufacture acquired by him when working earlier at the same craft in Haarlem and Amsterdam. A visitor to this works was John Evelyn, who recorded in his Diary on September 19th, 1676, that he had been there and saw '. . . looking-glasses far larger and better than any that come from Venice'. The Duke of Buckingham retired to live in Yorkshire in 1686, and his death took place in the following year.

In 1695, when William III had been on the throne six years and, in conjunction with the Dutch, was prosecuting a war against Louis XIV, it was decided by Parliament that the glass-industry should contribute its share towards the heavy expenses involved. 'Fine glass and looking-glass plates' were to have a Duty of 20 per cent levied and bottles of green glass a shilling a

---

[1] Robert Plot: *The Natural History of Oxfordshire*, 1677.
[2] John Dryden's celebrated lines in *Absolom and Achitophel*, staged in 1681, are bitingly satirical but probably very close to the mark:

> 'A man so various that he seemed to be
> Not one, but all mankind's epitome;
> Stiff in opinions, always in the wrong,
> Was everything by starts and nothing long;
> But, in the course of one revolving moon,
> Was chemist, fiddler, statesman and buffoon.
> Beggar'd by fools, whom still he found too late,
> He had his jest, but they had his estate.'

dozen, the tax to be applied only for a term of five years,[1] and a further Act, confirming the foregoing but making it permanent, was passed in 1696.[2] There was an immediate outcry as soon as the Duty was proposed, and a flood of petitions from all quarters, with the members of the Glass-sellers' Company in the forefront, reached Westminster. As a result, late in 1697 a Committee of the House of Commons was appointed to examine and report on the situation. Following its deliberations the Duty was halved in August, 1698,[3] abolished a year after,[4] and a tax-free period of almost fifty years was enjoyed.

The Vauxhall glasshouse continued in operation after the demise of its noble owner, although a lack of references to it may indicate that it was less active for a time. However, in 1700 the following advertisement appeared in *The Post Man* for February 13th:

'Large Looking-glass Plates, the like never made in England before, both for size and goodness, are now made at the old Glass House at Foxhall, known by the name of the Duke of Buckingham's House, Where all persons may be furnished with rough plates from the smallest sizes to those of six foot in length, and proportionable breadth, at reasonable rates.'[5]

Ten years later, the place was visited by Zacharias Conrad von Uffenbach, a German, who came to London for a stay of five months in which to study England and the English and to buy books. He recorded:

'On 21 July, Monday morning, we first went to see the porcelain sheds at Foxhall. . . . Next we went into the glass or mirror hut near by, where, fortunately, they happened just then to be blowing.'[6]

In 1691 a potential competitor had emerged, and the *London Gazette* printed the following in its issue of June 4–8th:

'There is now made at the Bear-Garden Glass-house on the Bankside Crown Window-Glass much exceeding French Glass in all its Qualification; which may be squared into all sizes of Sashes for Windows and other uses, and may be had at most Glasiers in London.'[5]

The range of productions was soon extended, and it is clear that the two glasshouses entered into competition with each other. *The Post Man*, the journal in which the Vauxhall works had advertised earlier (see above), printed this notice in its issue of January 13–15th, 1702;

'At the Bear Garden Glass-House in Southwrak (*sic*) are Looking-Glass Plates, Blown from the smallest size upwards, to 90 inches, with proportionable breadth, of lively Colours, free from Veins and foulness, incident to large Plates that have been hitherto sold.'

[1] 6 & 7 William and Mary, *c.* 18.   [2] 7 & 8 William III, *c.* 31.   [3] 9 William III, *c.* 45.
[4] 10 William III, *c.* 24. For this and the foregoing, see F. Buckley: *The Taxation of English Glass in the 17th Century*, privately printed, 1914.
[5] F. Buckley: *The Glass Trade in England in the 17th cty.*, privately printed, 1914, page 59.
[6] *London in 1710, from the Travels of Z. C. von Uffenbach*, translated and edited by W. H. Quarrell and Margaret Mare, 1934, page 132.

Confirmation that both of the preceding refer to the same establishment is provided in *The City and Countrey Purchaser*, published in 1703, in which the author wrote:[1]

'As to Looking-glass-plates, they are made at the Bear-garden on the Bankside, London. (where Crown-glass was 1st. made).'

The Bear Garden glasshouse soon ran into trouble with a prominent cabinet-maker, John Gumley (see page 152), who, in partnership with some city merchants, built a manufactory at Hungerford Market, Lambeth, expressly for the making of looking-glass. Petition followed petition to Parliament following an attempt by the Bear Garden proprietors to close Gumley's establishment. The former were accused of trying to corner the market, 'and thought they had so secured the Monopoly, that they put what Prizes they pleas'd upon the Home Consumption, and also upon what was exported; and refus'd to sell any *Glass-Plates* to Persons they thought were Enemies to their Monopoly, unless they would give Twenty Pounds *per cent* more than they were Sold for to others, to the great prejudice of the Trade.'[2] The answer was a firm denial of all the charges, and a postscript reading:

'Note, that Mr Gumley always did, and still does Sell Glass in his shop in the Strand, and the rest of his Partners are Merchants or Trades-men in the City, and none of them ever bred up in the Art or Mystery of making Glass; so that whether they, or the Proprietors of the *Bear-Garden Glass-House* (who have for several years last past imployed themselves and their Servants in finding out and Improving the said Art) are the Improvers of the same, and serve the Subjects best and cheapest . . . .'.[3]

In the end, the verbal battle faded away and Gumley's showroom received a mention from the pen of Sir Richard Steele, who printed a eulogistic description of *Mr Gumley's Glass Gallery over the New Exchange* in his periodical, *The Lover*.[4] John Gumley died in 1729; his retail business was carried on by his mother, and to his second son, John, he left his 'share in the business of Richard Hughes and Co., plate-glass manufacturers, Vauxhall'.

In 1745 the Chancellor of the Exchequer, Henry, Lord Pelham, imposed a Duty of 9s. 4d. on each hundredweight (cwt: 112 lb.) of ordinary glass and 2s. 4d. on each hundredweight of green bottle glass.[5] It was levied on the weight of material used in making articles, including sheet glass of any kind, and involved the attendance of Excise Officers at each glassworks for the purpose of weighing and calculating. Apart from the unpopularity of the tax itself, the method of assessment was highly inconvenient and eventually involved the licensing of each glasshouse at a charge of £10 a year.[6] It is not surprising to find that the consequent

---

[1] *The City and Countrey Purchaser, and Builder's Dictionary*, by T. N. (Probably written by Richard Neve), 1703, page 152.

[2] *The Case of Mr John Gumley and his Partners*, about 1706.

[3] *The Answer of the Proprietors of the Bear-Garden Glass-House*, about 1706.

[4] *The Lover, to which is added The Reader*, by Richard Steele, No. 34, 13th May, 1715.

[5] 19 George II, *c.* 12.   [6] In 1784.

outcry reached the journals of the time. A typical example is in the *Gentleman's Magazine* for March, 1746:

'Friday 5. A great number of men and women, who are occupiers of the glass trade, attended the house of commons with printed cases against the bill for laying a duty upon glass; containing in substance, that it will occasion some thousands of artisans, now employed in the following trades, viz. grinders, polishers, scallopers, file-beaters,[1] silverers, frame-makers, carvers, gilders, and gold-beaters, to be out of employment.'

This was followed by a brief notice, hardly a credible one and perhaps inspired by an eighteenth-century pressure-group:

'Saturday 29. Many of the glass-houses, of which there are but 40 in the kingdom, have discontinued working.'[2]

In spite of protests the Duty was continued, and in 1777 doubled to raise money for the war in America. In that year, also, a tax was levied on imported glass which would, as the Chancellor, Lord North, explained, 'be the means of keeping the glass-manufacture within the kingdom, the new duties on foreign importations being little short of a prohibition'. They amounted to 16d. per pound 'upon all enamelled, stained and paste glass, window-glass and glass-cakes imported', which compared with the home rate of 2d. per pound. The whole was calculated to produce a total sum of £45,000 a year, but this figure does not tally with the £71,749 which the lower Duty was said to have yielded in 1762.[3]

The Vauxhall Glassworks eventually came into the ownership of John Bowles and John Dawson who, with their successors, ran it during most of the eighteenth century. A brief history of the factory was given in *The History and Antiquities of Lambeth* by John Tanswell, published in 1858, where it is noted that 'about the year 1670, a number of Venetian artists arrived in England, the principal of whom was Rosetti; and, under the patronage of the Duke of Buckingham, a manufactory was established at Foxhall, and carried on with such amazing success, by the firm of Dawson, Bowles, and Co. . . . the emoluments acquired by the proprietors were prodigious, but in the year 1780, from a difference between them and the workmen, a total stop was put to this great acquisition and valuable manufactory, and a descendant of Rosetti ungratefully left in extreme poverty. The site of the celebrated factory is Vauxhall Square.' The continuance in operation of the works for a full period of one hundred years, as well as the widely recognised quality of its products, led to the acceptance of 'Vauxhall Glass' as an expression current to this day. It is not uncommon to find the term still used for mirror-glass of old appearance, although there may be no proof whatsoever of its place of origin.

Evidence of the cost of finished looking-glass in the middle years of the century, and the amount of Duty payable on it, was revealed in *The Plate-Glass-Book*, by 'A Glass-House

---

[1] File: tin-foil.   [2] Volume XVI, pages 161–2.
[3] John Campbell: *Political Survey of Great Britain*, 2 vols., 1774. Volume II, page 27, note f.

Clerk' (1757, and later editions). For a sheet measuring 60 by 42½ inches the charges were as follows:

Cost of rough plate	£37	10	0
Excise Duties	18	15	0
Grinding	7	12	8
Polishing	7	12	8
Silvering	7	12	8
Diamond-cutting	2	14	0

The total figure of £81 17s. would not have included a retailer's profit, and the final cost to the purchser doubtless exceeded £100.

In 1773 it was proposed to start making plate glass in England by the French casting process in use at Saint Gobain in Picardy. The method required premises of a much greater size, entirely different equipment, and a changed technique for its exploitation; the amount of capital needed to commence such an enterprise was calculated as being about £50,000. To protect themselves, the proprietors proposed the formation of a limited liability company, and for this purpose they sought incorporation by Act of Parliament. The matter was brought before the House, and duly reported in the *Gentleman's Magazine:*

'January 25. Mr Mackworth [Member of Parliament for Cardiff] presented a petition from a set of gentlemen, praying that they may be incorporated for the purpose of establishing a glass manufactory; and that the joint stock only, and not their private fortunes, may be subjected to the payment of their debts. This manufactory is for fabricating large glass plates, such as are imported from France, and valued at £400 to £500 each. The petition was referred to a committee.'[1]

The report of the Committee was accepted, a bill duly presented, and finally The British Cast Plate Glass Manufacturers was incorporated with factories in Southwark, London, and in Ravenhead, near St Helens, Lancashire.[2]

The original proprietors proposed were to include two members of the Mackay family, one of whom, John, had business connections with Cheshire salt-works. From these, he had

[1] Volume XLVIII, page 98. The report of the Committee, presented to the House a month later, on 24th February, is of sufficient interest to merit reprinting in full and it will be found at the end of this book as Appendix 1, page 129.

[2] Under the Act of 13 Geo. III c. 38, the company was allowed to raise £40,000 in £500 shares and a further £20,000 if three-fourths of the proprietors agreed, and corporate rights for twenty-one years were obtained. The original proprietors were named as: Charles Fitzroy, the Hon. Robert Digby, Peregrine Cust, Thomas Dundas, John Mackay, Philip Affleck, Henry Dagge, James Bourdieu, Angus Mackay, Henry Hastings, Ranald Macdonald and Samuel Chollet. By the time the company was actually incorporated, the last two no longer figured and their places were taken by some important personages including: the third Earl of Bute, Major-General Fitzroy (later, first Baron Southampton), Herbert (later, Sir Herbert) Mackworth of a Cardiff family with big interest in copper-smelting, Thomas Patten, a Warrington copper-smelter, and Sir Robert Palk, former Governor of Madras and owner of extensive properties in Devonshire. See T. C. Barker and J. R. Harris, *op. cit.*, page 108 *et seq.*

extended his interests in the locality to embrace the coal essential for salt-making, and developed some important coal-mines. He has been named as the man responsible for the creation of the industrial area of St Helens and Ravenhead, and in seeking outlets for coal surplus to his salt-work activities was able to attract to the district the smelting works of the fabulous Welsh Parys Mountain copper-mine. In the same way, he was doubtless interested in starting a fresh coal-using trade that would come to the area, and there can be little doubt that it was due to Mackay, a Scotsman living in London in 1761 when he first became interested in the north-west, that the glass company came to Ravenhead.[1]

The company built a casting-hall which was then the largest industrial building in the country, and the first sheet of glass was produced there in 1776. When, in 1788, she visited Osterley Park, then the seat of the widow of Robert Child, Mrs Philip Lybbe Powys noted in the principal bedroom 'the first plate made in England'.[2] Robert Adam prepared plans for Osterley and its contents over a period of some twenty years between 1761 and 1780, and his designs for the bedstead and bedcover in Mrs Child's English Bedroom, as it was called, are dated 1775-7. It is not at all improbable that one of the looking-glasses remaining in the room to this day is the very plate that initiated the activities of the Ravenhead factory.[3]

A Frenchman, Philip Besnard, who had given evidence before the Committee in 1773, disappeared from the scene, and casting began under the control of a compatriot, Jean Baptiste François Graux de la Bruyère, born at Saint Gobain, who remained in charge until he died in 1787. The difficulties inseparable from a new, large-scale undertaking were slow in being overcome, and a further burden in 1781 took the form of a rise in Duty: 'All excisable commodities, beer, malt, soap and leather excepted' were subjected to a further 5 per cent. Also, it must be remembered that the existing Duty (9s. 4d. per cwt on other than green glass) had been doubled in 1777, only a year after the factory had begun work. These factors led to steadily mounting debts, and in 1784 casting was brought to a complete standstill. Apart from the minor activity of blowing small-sized plates, the idleness lasted for at least a year during which the company reiterated bitterly the complaint that its troubles were due to over-taxation: no uncommon cry at any time. Duty being levied in the normal manner by weight of raw material, it was found that the percentage of waste in casting had been grossly miscalculated, and the amount of finished glass obtainable from a given quantity of taxed raw material was noticeably less than could be got by blowing.

A Parliamentary Committee was set up to inquire into the matter, agreed that the complaint was well founded, and gave their opinion that 'the plate glass manufacturers had paid £7,000 more duty than was intended by the legislature'. After failing to get this sum refunded, which was refused as a matter of principle, it was moved 'that the duty on plate glass ought

---

[1] *Passages from the Diaries of Mrs Philip Lybbe Powys*, ed. Emily J. Climenson, 1899, page 231.

[2] *Ibid.*, page 112.

[3] This is the famous bed castigated by Horace Walpole on account of its crowning festoons of artificial flowers: 'The bed is . . . too like a modern head-dress. . . . What would Vitruvius think of a dome decorated by a milliner?' Letter to the Rev. W. Mason, 16th July, 1778.

to be collected on the weight of glass after it is squared', and this was agreed in 1787.[1] In the same year, a tax of 1s. 5½d. a square foot was levied on imported French plate, with comparable amounts on other glass products from the same source, which seems to show that the Duty of ten years earlier was not proving as prohibitive as forecast at the time by the Chancellor.

Manufacture recommenced and efforts were made to improve the company's financial position. Wastage was considerably lessened, and it was realised that profits might be increased if the glass was sold in the polished state rather than as it left the table. In May, 1790, an agreement was made with George and Matthew Kemp of London, who were 'possessed of a valuable Secret or Invention for making and constructing Mills and Machines for grinding and Polishing Plate Glass . . . there being nothing equal to it, they [the Kemps] believe, in the World'.[2] At about the same date negotiations were under way with James Watt for the installation of one of his steam engines for the same purpose. All this took time, and the Kemps' polishing process did not come into use before 1792, in which year a new manager, Robert Sherbourne, was appointed.

In 1794 application was made to the House of Commons for a renewed charter of incorporation, the original having run its allotted twenty-one years, but although the Bill was passed it did not receive the concurrence of the Lords.[3] The concern was then continued as an unincorporated company by the original proprietors aided by a London man, Thomas Oakes, who arranged with them to buy it for £105,000. Then, in 1798, a further application for a Bill was successful[4] and the concern was known henceforth as the British Plate Glass Company. It prospered, and by 1801 was producing more than 7,000 plates a year together with proportionate profits. The campaigns of Napoleon ensured that the intense competition suffered from

---

[1] *Gentleman's Magazine*, vol. LV, part ii, page 623. 17 Geo. III, *c*. 28. In 1794 the duty was again levied on the weight of materials used. *Journal H. of C.*, 49, page 349 (18th March, 1794).

The law and its application had reached a complicated state by 1790: 'The act of 27 Geo. III recites also that, in lieu of the duty of excise on the materials for making Cast Plate-Glass in Great Britain, which was formerly £1 1s. 5½d., the same duty is now to be paid on that article *when manufactured*, provided the thickness of all such Cast Plate-Glass shall be as follows; viz: 10-20th-parts of an inch at least in thickness, if such superficial contents of such shall be 6147 square inches and upwards; 9-20th-parts at least thick, if 6147, and not less than 5215; 8-20th-parts if under 5125, and not less than 4282; 7-20th-parts 4282, and not less than 3350; 6-20th-parts if under 3350, and not less than 2417; 5-20th if 2417, and not less than 1485, square inches.

'In the city of *London*, the officer must have *six* hours notice, in writing, when the plates are to be drawn out of the annealing arch; and, in any other part of Great Britain, *twelve* hours. Said plates to be squared, and the mullet, or cuttings, arising therefrom, weighed in the presence of the officer, on penalty of £50. If the Glass be not squared in an hour after an officer attends, he is to charge the duty as on the *materials*, viz. £1 1s. 5½d. at which rate he is to make a charge on the *materials* in every case where the plates do not weigh 2-3rds of the weight of such materials. All Plate-Glass not squared into plates, is to be broken into small pieces; and no Plate-Glass shall be removed before the duty has been charged thereon; for each of these offences against the act, the maker forfeits £50.' *The Universal British Directory*, 1790, pages 761–2.

[2] *Objections on the Part of Messieurs Kemp to the Bill for Dissolving the Plate Glass Manufactory, Corporation, &c.*, April, 1794. See p. 154.

[3] *Journal of the House of Commons*, vol. LIX (1794), pages 413, 467 and 570.

[4] Barker and Harris, *op. cit.*, page 115. 38 Geo. III, *c*. XVII.

Saint Gobain was no longer to be feared, and the home market was supplied almost exclusively with English plate. In addition, soon afterwards exportation was attempted and consignments were sent to the United States, India and elsewhere. After more than a century's trading, in 1901, the company was absorbed by the present renowned firm of Pilkington Brothers: descendants of William Pilkington of St Helens, who had left the family wine and spirit business in 1828 to manage the newly-opened St Helens Crown Glass Works.

In 1812 the duty on glass was raised again, but in 1832 a reduction was made and, finally, after a duration of just one hundred years since its imposition, it was abolished altogether in 1845. The industry was free at last to grapple with its problems without glancing over its shoulder at the tax-gatherer; during the majority of the period covered by this volume his menacing figure was present and the levying of a tax, especially one that increased as the years wore on, must have hindered progress in many ways in every glasshouse. In spite of duties that came and went, and rose and fell, the manufacturers overcame the challenges of imports from both Venice and France, and the name of Vauxhall remains current (obstinately, and usually incorrectly) as their memorial.

2

The Composition and Manufacture of Looking-glass Plates

It was related by Pliny that glass was invented accidentally by some Phoenician merchants camping at a river mouth in Syria. They were using some of their ship's cargo of natron to support a cooking-pot over the fire, and found that the heat had made the sand form glass. Both the time and the place of the romantic story have been doubted, but the other facts are not improbable: natron is an impure carbonate of soda, and, basically, glass is silica (in the form of sand, flint or quartz) which fuses in heat with the aid of a flux of potash or soda. In practice, other ingredients are added and there are, and have been, many different formulae for different purposes, each maker preferring his own private variation.

In England, we are indebted for the knowledge of the processes of glass-making, as regards a printed source, to the work of an Italian, Antonio Neri, whose *L'Arte Vetraria*, published in Florence in 1612, was rendered into English as *The Art of Glass* fifty years later. The translator was Dr Christopher Merret, a member of the Royal Society and a learned man of his time, who added a commentary of his own to the work. The dictionaries and encyclopaedias of the arts and sciences that began to appear in the late seventeenth century were seldom original in their content, and few of their compilers acknowledged the sources of their information. As regards glass, many of them gave lengthy instructions for its manufacture based on Neri *via* Merret, but which smack as much of alchemy as of practical experience. Others offered so many alternatives, both of ingredients and of time and method, that they are equally confusing to follow.

Typical of the early instructions were those of William Salmon in his *Polygraphice*.[1] He began a chapter entitled 'Of Salts for Glass Works', by stating that he did not propose to discourse on the actual making of glass, but to deal only with some of the ingredients. This he did at length and with references to classical authors in support of his statements. After three pages devoted to Salts, he continued with 'Of making Frit for Crystals':

'To make this *Frit*, you must have a great quantity of *Tarso* which is a matter fusible, and capable of being rendered white and transparent by force of Fire: and this Matter is either white or transparent Sand, or some sorts of Stones. . . . The *Venetians* and *Italians* make Glass in the Isle of *Muran* of a white *Flint*, which they have out of the River *Ticinus*, where there is a vast quantity of them: and they are found also in the River *Arnus*, both above and below *Florence*. . . . And it is true, that all white and transparent Stones, which will not become Lime, are fit for making Glass: these, and all Fire Stones, and those which will strike Fire, when they are calcined and reduced to an impalpable Pouder, and sifted thro' a very fine Sieve, will make a most admirable fine and pure *Crystal*. But the Art is to reduce the *Tarso* to such a fine and impalpable Pouder, the Trouble of which has caused the Glass-men to give it off, and to use, in the place of it, pure white fine Sand, because there is little or no Expence in its Preparation, it needing only washing clean, drying and sifting.'

Salmon pointed out that flints had been found to produce a better material than sand, and then gave this alternative formula:

'*Tarso* prepared, or fine white Crystaline Sand   lb xx
Salt of *Pulverine*[2]   lb xiii

mix well together, put them into a Furnace to be calcined, making the Fire gentle the first hour, and continually stirring it with an Iron Rake, that the Ingredients may the better incorporate.'

After continued heating, stirring and testing, the mixture was eventually removed from the heat and cooled. Then it was crushed and stored before being incorporated as an ingredient of the final product.

Half a century later, secrets were less closely guarded or authors were better informed, and

---

[1] *Polygraphice; or, The Arts of Drawing, Limning, Painting, &c.,* 1672; quotations are taken from the eighth edition, 1701, page 734. The author is described in the *Dictionary of National Biography* as 'empiric; travelled in various countries as mountebank', which does not recommend him as an authority particularly to be trusted. In the Preface he states that fifteen thousand copies of the first seven editions of the *Polygraphice* had been sold during thirty years. This would amount to 500 copies per annum and does not seem to be an unreasonable figure at that period; it implies that Salmon's contemporaries had a respect for the merits of the volume.

[2] Ash containing a high proportion of soda, obtained from a burned marine plant. It was imported from Spain, where it was known as *barilla*, and in the form of lumps, called *rochetta*, from Syria, Egypt and the Levant.

Robert Dossie prefaced a section on glass in the second volume of his *Handmaid to the Arts*[1] with a clear and stern warning:

'The glass for forming the looking-glass plates in perfection is the most nice and difficult to manage, of any whatever; there being no latitude with respect to several of the qualities, as there is in the case of flint-glass, without its goodness being really impaired.'

He was far more explicit on the subject than Salmon had been, and gave the following formula:

'*Best composition of glass for looking-glass plates*: Take of white sand cleansed sixty pounds, of purified pearl-ashes[2] twenty five pounds, of salt-petre fifteen pounds, and of borax seven pounds.'

In addition, he wrote: 'This composition is not to be made without expence, at the times when borax is dear: but the great price which looking-glass plates, particularly such as are large, bear, will very well allow it: or even the adding a greater quantity of borax, when there is occasion to have the glass run more easily, and roll in a less degree of heat.'

Of the actual furnace it was noted elsewhere: 'The furnace is of very large dimensions, environed with several ovens, or annealing furnaces, called carquasses, besides others for making of frit, and calcining old pieces of glass. This furnace, before it is fit to run glass, costs three thousand five hundred pounds. It seldom lasts above three years, and even in that time it must be refitted every six months. It takes six months to rebuild it; and three months to refit it. The melting pots are as big as large hogsheads, and contain about 2,000 weight of metal. If one of them bursts in the furnace, the loss of the matter and time amounts to £250. The heat of the furnace is so intense, that a bar of iron laid at the mouth thereof becomes red hot in less than half a minute.'[3] Another writer noted the difficulty of replacing a worn or cracked melting-pot, adding: 'But before they set about this rough work, those who do it clothe themselves in a sort of skins in the shape of a pantaloon, which they make as wet as possible, and which covers them all over except the eyes; and for them they make use of glass to see to guide themselves.'[4]

The formation of flat plates suitable for looking-glass was performed in two ways: by the Lorraine or 'broad' process, or by casting. The first-named was ingenious, and in view

[1] *The Handmaid to the Arts*, 2 volumes, 1758; second edition, 1764. Issued anonymously, it is accepted generally that the compiler was Robert Dossie, an active member of the Society for the Encouragement of Arts, Manufactures and Commerce, later the Royal Society of Arts, and a man who enjoyed the esteem of Dr Johnson.

[2] Potassium carbonate: a form of potash.

[3] *The Complete Dictionary of Arts and Sciences*, by the Rev. T. H. Croker, Thomas Williams and Samuel Clark, 3 vols., 1768. The figures given were 'lifted' from the *Dictionarium Polygraphicum* of 1735, and possibly have an even earlier origin. In spite of this, and their consequent inapplicability nearly fifty years later, they were given, without a source being named, by John Campbell in *The Political Survey of Great Britain* (1774), to show that 'It requires a great Fortune to embark in making Plate Glass'. Most of the dictionaries and encyclopaedias give instructions, varying in detail, for building furnaces.

[4] *Dictionarium Polygraphicum: Or The Whole Body of Arts Regularly Digested*; published anonymously in two volumes in 1735; but probably compiled by John Barrow. The garment described as being 'in the shape of a pantaloon' would seem to have been a forerunner of the modern boiler-suit plus a head-covering.

of the somewhat complicated technique involved it is probably remarkable to modern readers that it should have been developed and remained in general use in this country for fully a century and a half. It required the preliminary to all blown glass manufactures: the charging of the blow-pipe with molten 'metal' and the blowing of a bubble from it. The latter was then manipulated until it was sausage-shaped, the ends were cut off, and the resulting tube slit along its length and opened out flat. Finally, it was placed in an annealing oven to cool very slowly before it was handled further. Its drawback was that there was a limit to the size of sheet that could be made by it.

Casting meant what the name implies: the molten glass was poured on to a flat metal-topped table with low sides of the height of the finished plate, the mass was smoothed by means of a metal bar resting on the sides and annealing followed.

The 'broad' process must have needed craftsmen of considerable skill and experience for its management. It was claimed that plates 82 by 48 inches in size could be made by the process,[1] and these would have entailed the feat of blowing and controlling a 'bubble' 48 inches in length by about 27 inches in diameter. It must be pointed out, however, that the blowing was not performed in one mighty 'puff', but the growing glass sphere was returned constantly to the mouth of the furnace to reheat and retain its plasticity between bouts of expansion and elongation. The *Dictionarium Polygraphicum*[2] warns its readers that blown plates should not be more than 48 or 50 inches in length 'and proportionable in breadth. Those which exceed these dimensions, as has been frequently experienced in those of Venetian make, cannot have a thickness sufficient to bear the grinding, and besides are subject to warp, which causes them to be false, hindering them from regularly reflecting the objects.'

Until the mid-1770s the 'broad' process was in use generally in England, and few or no attempts were made to compete with the large-sized sheets imported first from Venice and then from France. The demand for these was sufficient and the price and quality were attractive enough to outweigh the sporadic prohibitions of importation and the gradual raising of Duty that took place over the years. It is probable that such prohibitions were often ignored and the Duty evaded, and there was doubtless just as much smuggling of glass as of tea, lace, chinaware, and much else.

At this point, it may be apposite to quote some contemporary observers of the 'broad' process, and note a few of the announcements of manufacturers who used it. The earliest in this latter category is the statement of 1621 that Sir Robert Mansell made looking-glass 'wch was never wont to be in England before', and the Venetian Ambassador's letter of 1620[3] mentions that looking-glasses were being made in the country to which he was accredited. Mansell had obtained his patent of monopoly in 1615, and although we have no certainty of knowing whether suitable glass plates were not being manufactured here before that date, it may be

[1] In evidence given before a Parliamentary Committee in 1773 by a 'Mr Bowles' (? of Vauxhall). The Duke of Buckingham's glasshouse advertised plates 72 inches long in 1700, and two years later the Bear Garden glasshouse announced plates up to 90 inches (see pages 45 and 132).

[2] *Op cit*. Volume II, under *Looking Glass*.   [3] See page 42.

queried whether they could have been produced on a commercially successful scale without some mention of the fact having been preserved.

The first eye-witness report is that of the diarist John Evelyn in September, 1676, who had visited the glassworks on the isle of Murano in 1645, and sent home 'a collection of divers curiosities and glasses'. Then, thirty-one years later, he wrote, after seeing the Duke of Buckingham's establishment, that they made there 'looking-glasses far larger and better than any that come from Venice'; a surprising statement that seems to smack more of patriotism than of truth. This is not unlikely to have been the case, for at the time there was considerable activity to conserve currency and make England less dependent on imports. Equally, of course, advances and changes in techniques since Evelyn had been to Murano must have been considerable, and he may have been comparing what he saw in 1676 with what he remembered having seen three decades earlier.

The Southwark Bear Garden glasshouse advertised 'Looking-Glass Plates, Blown . . .', in 1702, and the eye-witness account of Zacharias Conrad von Uffenbach in 1710 leaves no doubt of the process in use at Vauxhall.[1] After remarking that it is 'uncommonly hot work, and the blowing very arduous', he continues: 'First they take out a great mass, which they repeatedly blow up in a circle and then again make red-hot; when it is large enough they take it to the so-called "pulpit", which is really a chair raised on several steps, below which a man stands with a pair of scissors and cuts the great bubble in pieces; then it is laid on a large sheet of iron, on which the glass is stretched. On this it is placed in the cooling oven and smoothed out with an iron resembling a scraper; then it is stood in an upright position and left for three days to cool. Then the panes are sold to other people who cut and mount them, making mirrors of them; this is a special trade followed by many people in London.'

The casting of glass plates is thought to have been known to the Romans, but it is doubtful whether they made pieces of any considerable size by the method. The more modern employment of the process dates from the year 1687, when it was reinvented in France by an Italian-born glass-maker, Bernard Perrot, in 1687. A Frenchman, Louis-Lucas de Nehou, realised the possibilities of the process, and with the financial help of Abraham Thévart, a Paris lawyer, and his friends, a factory was opened in the Faubourg St Antoine. Manufacture commenced in 1691, and 'il presenta au roi [Louis XIV] les quatre premières coulées. A partir de ce jour, cette fabrication ne cessa plus jamais'.[2] In the following year, in order to lower costs, the factory removed to St Gobain in Picardy.

Dr Lister, visiting the French capital in 1698, recorded the following: 'The Glass-house out of the Gate of St Antoine well deserves seeing: but I did lament the Fondery was no longer there, but removed to Cherborne in Normandy for cheapness of fuel. 'Tis certainly a most considerable addition to the Glass-making. For I saw here one Looking-glass foiled and finisht, 88 inches long, and 48 inches broad; and yet but one quarter of an inch thick. This, I think,

[1] Op. cit., page 132. See page 45.
[2] Comte Elphège Frémy: Histoire de la manufacture Royale des Glaces de France au XVIIe et au XVIIIe siècle, Paris, 1909.

could never be effected by the Blast of any Man; but I suppose to be run or cast upon sand, as Lead is; which yet, I confess, the toughness of Glass Mettal makes very much against.'[1]

Undoubtedly, casting was practised successfully in France, but blowing was used there also. Probably the former was confined to the making of large sheets, whereas the latter was more economical when smaller looking-glasses were required. Both processes are described and illustrated in the great eighteenth-century *Encyclopédie*.[2]

In England, a patent was granted in 1691 to 'Robert Hooke, Esquire, and Christopher Dodsworth, Merchant,' for various improvements in glass-making, and for 'the art of casting glasse, and particularly looking glasse plates, much larger than ever was blowne in England or foreigne parts'. It appears to be unrecorded whether the granting of this patent resulted in actual manufacture, and it may well have borne no more fruit than some of Hooke's innumerable other inventions.[3]

William Salmon, writing in 1701, gave instructions for casting which are clear and concise. He gave no details of any other process, and unfortunately did not comment on this one; he printed the following:

'The substance or Metal of Looking-Glasses, is to be Crystal Frit or Frit made of Flints; the melted Matter of which is to be cast upon an excellently polisht Table of pure tough Copper or Iron; which Table must be of the Magnitude you desire, and its bottom so much sunk as you intend the thickness of your Glass Plate to be, *viz.* it is to have Edges round about it so high as your Glass is to be thick: over this you are to have a Plate or Runner of Metal, to slide and press it on the melted Glass, that it may spread itself all over the Copper or Iron Table, to make it close, compact and even.'[4]

A further reference to casting in the first half of the eighteenth century occurs in the *Dictionarium Polygraphicum* (1735), which gives details of it and concludes: 'This art is said to be of French invention, and not yet of 60 years standing, being owing to the Sieur Abraham Thevart, who first propos'd it to the Court of France in the year 1688; but has been considerably improv'd by our workmen in England'.[5] These words certainly imply that casting was then being, or had been, practised in this country.

---

[1] *A Journey to Paris in the Year 1698*, by Dr Martin Lister, 1699. Martin Lister, F.R.S. (1638?–1712), accompanied the Earl of Portland on an embassy to Paris following the Treaty of Ryswick. He contributed extensively to the *Philosophical Transactions* of the Royal Society, and was medical adviser to Queen Anne.

[2] Published in Paris between 1751 and 1780 under the general editorship of Diderot, it ran to a total of 35 folio volumes.

[3] Dr Robert Hooke (1635–1703) was for a while Secretary of the Royal Society and for forty years their Curator of Experiments. He is remembered for his successful work in connection with the wheel- or dial-barometer and for several important horological inventions.

[4] *Polygraphice* (*op. cit.*), page 849.

[5] Both blowing and casting are described in this work. Under the heading 'Grinding Glass' appears the following sentence: 'In the new method of working large plates of Glass for looking glasses &c. by moulding, and as it were casting them somewhat after the manner of metals. . . .' Although the writer here refers to casting as 'the new method' he does not state that it is actually in use, and the word 'new' may have been used in the sense of 'different'.

Tantalisingly slight evidence was given many years later before the Parliamentary Committee of 1773. A Mr Bowles then stated that he had on his premises a piece of cast glass measuring 100 inches in length by 40 inches wide. He no longer produced his plates by the method of casting, the apparatus for which had been 'long since destroyed'. On the same occasion a Mr Dickson gave evidence that 'at Mr Cookson's Manufactory for Plate Glass, the largest size made in 84 by 50 inches, which he believes were cast'.[1]

After so much uncertainty on the subject, it is some comfort to reach the year 1773 in which there is the first unshakeable evidence that the process was, or was about to be, in use. As mentioned earlier, the British Cast Plate Glass Manufacturers then came into being, and although blowing continued to be employed until some time in the nineteenth century it was gradually supplanted. One other firm that certainly used casting deserves a mention: the bill-head of George Seddon and Son records that in addition to being 'Cabinet-makers and Upholders' they were 'also Manufacturers of British Cast Large Plate Glass'.[2] This bears out the words of Sophie von la Roche, a German novelist who was in London during 1786, and recorded in her diary a visit to the firm's premises in Aldersgate Street. She concluded her description with the words: 'In the basement mirrors are cast and cut'.[3]

Apart from the limit in the size of plates that could be blown by the 'broad' process compared with those that could be cast, the appearance of the final products was identical. The question of which process was used and when, while it is of interest both historically and technically, is only an academic one. Even when, on account of its size, it can be decided with certainty by which process a particular piece of glass must have been made, there arises the question of whether it was cast in this country or not. The imposition of higher import Duties in 1777 and 1787 must be accepted as proof that French plates continued to be sent across the Channel, and that the success of their English competitors was not instantaneous.

There was a further method of making sheet glass, known as the 'Crown' process, which merits mention. In this, a bubble of glass was blown, flattened and then with swift rotation formed into a circle of large diameter. Where it was broken from the tool, a mark similar to that beneath an old wine-glass, known as a 'pontil-mark', remained, and it is this central section that was used for making so-called 'Bull's Eye' windows. The outer portions of the sheet were cut into sizes suitable for glazing windows, but the surface was furrowed and ridged in the making. It was too thin to stand grinding flat, and usually would not have been strong enough to withstand the weights normally applied for silvering.

'Crown' glass was sold by the case of 'tables', each table being a sheet averaging three to four feet in diameter, and the contents of a case varying with each manufactory. Much of it was made in London before 1700 at the Bear Garden glasshouse in Southwark. Richard Neve

---

[1] See Appendix 1, page 129.

[2] A bill-head dated 1790 is reproduced in *Old English Furniture*, issued by M. Harris & Sons, London, in 1935. The account is for furniture supplied to D. Tupper, Esq., Hauteville House, Guernsey, Channel Islands, and the printed wording 'Geo. Seddon & Son' was altered in 1790 to read 'Geo. Seddon Sons & Shackleton'. See page 157.

[3] *Sophie in London, 1786*, translated from the German by Clare Williams, 1933, page 174.

pointed out three years later: 'But now at the *Bear-garden Looking-glass plates* are made; the maker of this best sort of *Crown-glass*, being now removed to *Ratcliffe*, and upon that account it now bears the Name of *Ratcliff Crown-glass* . . . I have been told by some *London Glaziers* that there is 24 Tables of this *Crown-glass* to the *Case*, the *Tables* being of a circular Form, of about 3 Foot, 6 or 8 Inches Diameter, and by consequence, each *Table* will be in Area about 9 or 10 Foot, and the *Case* betwixt 220 and 240 Foot'.[1]

In the second half of the eighteenth century 'Crown' glass was used sometimes for the making of Chinese 'mirror-pictures', but the distorted surface of the material spoilt their effect.[2]

[1] *The City and Countrey Purchaser, and Builder's Dictionary*, by T. N., 1703, pages 149–50.
[2] See Appendix 2, page 137.

3

Grinding, Polishing, Diamonding and Foiling of Plates

As was noted by von Uffenbach when he was in London in 1710, the glass-makers did no more than manufacture the material, 'then the panes are sold to other people who cut and mount them, making mirrors of them; this is a special trade followed by many people in London'.[1] Perhaps in a few instances all processes of manufacture were carried out on the same premises, but there are entries in eighteenth-century Directories of such tradesmen as Glass-grinders, who would have ground, polished and bevelled, and Looking-glass Manufacturers, who would have performed the operation of silvering.

When it finally left the annealing oven the sheet of glass was far from being perfectly smooth if made by the 'broad' process, and if cast would be equally unfit for immediate use. In both cases, unevenness at the edges was trimmed off, and the maximum area of glass left for further processes. A practical manufacturer wrote: 'Although the plate is flat, the surfaces of the plate, owing to the contact of the hot glass with the air, the casting plate, and the roller, are ruffled, and the glass is translucent but not transparent'.[2]

[1] *Op. cit.*, page 132.   [2] Harry J. Powell, *Glassmaking in England*, Cambridge, 1923, page 123.

Both grinding and polishing, to which a sheet of glass was subjected, were essentially the same: whereas the former removed visible marks and excrescences, the latter produced a final shining surface. Grinding employed abrasives of varying coarseness according to the amount of work to be done, and the need to leave as smooth a surface as possible. Polishing was performed with increasingly fine and soft powders until the final perfection was attained.

The scene in a Paris workshop in 1698 was described by Martin Lister, and doubtless it changed little there or in England during the course of the following century. He wrote:

'There they are polished; which imploys daily 600 Men, and they hope in a little time to employ a 1000 in several Galleries. In the lower they grind the course Glass with a Sand Stone, the very same they pave the Streets in *Paris*; of which broken they have great heaps in the Courts of the Work-Houses: This Stone is beat to Powder, and sifted through a fine Tamis. In the Upper Gallery, where they polish and give the last Hand, they work in 3 Rowes, and 2 Men at a Plate, with Ruddle and Powdered Haematites in Water.

'The Glasses are set fast in White Puttie, upon flat Tables of Stone, sawed thin for that purpose. The grinding the Edges and Borders is very troublesome, and odious for the horrid grating noise it makes, and which cannot be endured to one that is not used to it; and yet by long custom these Fellows are so easie with it, that they Discourse together as nothing were. This is done below, and out of the way of the rest.'[1]

A later description refers to a grinder made from a small-sized sheet of rough glass cemented to a weighted piece of wood, which was pushed about on top of the plate to be ground, and kept supplied with liberal applications of sand and water between the surfaces. For very large sheets a wheel was fixed horizontally to the top of the grinder, and this was pushed back and forth and moved around by two men standing opposite one another.

As early as 1678 a patent was granted to John Roberts 'for his invention of grinding, polishing and diamonding glass plates for looking glasses, etc., by the motion of water and wheels',[2] and in 1696 a patent for another method was granted to Thomas Savery, better known for his work on the steam-engine. Two years later, in 1698, the *London Gazette* advertised a comparable machine in use at 'Mr Richard Robinson's at the Flower-Pot in Beaufort Street in the Strand'.[3] This or another device caused William Salmon to make the following comment: 'All these things [grinding, polishing and cutting] were formerly done by Hand; but now Art is come to that Perfection, that what was formerly performed with vast Labor and Pains, besides an almost invincible Care, is now performed easily, and exactly, and as it were at once, by the help of an admirable *Engine* or *Mill*, out-doing the operation by the Hands, almost a thousand fold.'[4] In spite of this apparently complete success a notice in the *Tatler* of 19th April, 1710, stated that trading at the *Flower-Pot* was to be discontinued, the stock disposed of, and 'no more of the Engine-Work to be had after this Sale'. A patent was granted in 1718 'for Grinding Looking-Glass, Colours, Polishing of Marble, &c.', and doubtless there

[1] *Op. cit.*, page 141.   [2] Patent of 5th June, 1678—No. 203.
[3] Issue of 14–17th November, 1698.   [4] *Polygraphice*, pages 849–50.

were others.[1] About 1760, a further machine, designed by 'Mr Burroughs of Southwark', was awarded a premium of £70 by the recently-formed Society of Arts, and was illustrated and described in detail in *The Complete Dictionary of Arts and Sciences*, 1764.[2] There is no evidence that any of these attempts at mechanisation were successful, but in 1786–90 James Watt applied himself to the problem of polishing the plates cast at Ravenhead and one of his steam engines was installed for the purpose.[3]

In the words of an eighteenth-century writer: 'After looking-glasses have been ground, they are to be polished, they still looking but something like a slate. The polishing is perform'd in the following manner: the plate is laid down on a stone plac'd horizontally, and, in a bed of plaister of *Paris* calcin'd and pulveris'd very fine and sifted; which being made into a sort of paste by water, and plaister'd up the edges of the plate, dries and hardens, and so keeps it immoveable; then the workman fixing a strong bow of yew or some other tough wood, to a board fixed up to the ceiling of the room, fixes also the other end into a hole made in a wooden parallelopepid of about four inches long, cover'd with a sort of coarse woollen cloth well drench'd with *Tripoly*, tempered with water, works it with this block and bow all over by strength of arm, till the plates has got a perfect politure.'[4] The ingenious use of a wooden 'spring' eased the task of the workman, and took some of the back-ache out of the job.

Dr Johnson, when he was in Paris in company with Mr and Mrs Thrale and Joseph Baretti, visited the looking-glass manufactory on Monday, 23rd October, 1775. He remarked that the plates were cast in Normandy, and that those he saw were as much as a third of an inch in thickness. His descriptions of the actual grinding and polishing processes varied little from those given earlier by Lister, but he referred to the spring-loaded polishing block as 'a contrivance which I did not well understand'. He mentioned the fact that after being ground flat, the plates were left rough-surfaced until they were sold, and only then did they receive their final polish and silvering. In that way, accidental damage was avoided.[5]

Diamonding and diamond-cutting are the old terms for what is called nowadays bevelling: making the edge of the plate of glass angled slightly from the plane. It was ground to shape in the same way as the flat front and back of the sheet, and finished similarly by polishing. Early eighteenth-century diamonding was often so slight as scarcely to be felt with the finger, and the surface rounded rather than angled. This subtle bevel is often taken to be a true sign of age and the hallmark of 'genuine Vauxhall', but it can be, and has been, imitated successfully. Modern glass is finished with a neat sharply-angled bevel that is not found on old pieces. Bevelling of looking-glass plates was fashionable from the late seventeenth century onwards, but the mode for it was not continuous, and hard-and-fast rules as to whether it was used or not at

[1] *London Gazette*, No. 5654, 24th June, 1718.

[2] Volume I under *Burrough's Machine*, and plate 27. In 1767 the Society paid Jeremiah Burrows £20 for a model of his machine.

[3] T. C. Barker and J. R. Harris, *op. cit.*, page 115, footnote 3.

[4] *Dictionarium Polygraphicum*, 1735. Tripoly or Tripoli: a fine earth used for polishing.

[5] *The Works of Samuel Johnson*, Yale edition, 1958 *et. seq.*, vol. I, page 243; *Boswell's Life of Johnson*, ed. L. F. Powell, Oxford, 1934–50, vol. II, page 396.

certain dates cannot be laid down. A writer of 1760 noted: 'it is not usual, of late, to Diamond-cut the Edges of Glasses put into French Frames': i.e. rococo frames.[1]

The actual silvering of sheet glass was known as foiling, foliating and, occasionally, as filing. The most detailed contemporary directions for performing the process appeared in the *Dictionarium Polygraphicum:*

'A thin blotting paper is spread on a table, and sprinkled with fine chalk; and then a fine *lamina* or leaf of tin, called *foil*, is laid over the paper; upon this *mercury* is poured, which is equally to be distributed over the leaf with a hare's foot or cotton. Over the leaf is laid a clean paper, and over that the glass plate.

'The glass plate is press'd down with the right hand, and the paper is drawn gently out with the left; which being done, the plate is covered with a thicker paper, and loaden with a greater weight, that the superfluous *mercury* may be driven out, and the *tin* adhere more closely to the glass.

'When it is dried, the weight is removed, and the looking-glass is complete.'[2]

The writer mentions that sometimes melted marcasite is added to the mercury and, with this, others include a little lead and tin 'so that the glass may dry the sooner'.

Bevelled plates needed slightly different treatment. A table was prepared with adjustable raised angle-pieces to fit against the bevel when the glass was laid face-downwards on it. The tin-foil and the mercury were applied to the back, which lay uppermost, then sheets of paper were followed by weights. Unless the supporting angle-pieces were fitted to the shape of the bevels, the latter would be broken as the mercury was squeezed out. Alternatively, whether bevelled or not, the plate was raised very slowly from the horizontal—a matter of inches a day —to let the surplus run off, and until the silvering had dried. Johnson saw this being done in Paris in 1775, and noted 'the slope is daily heightened towards a perpendicular'.

The eighteenth-century glass-grinders received few mentions in their day, but although many remained anonymous Thomas Mortimer gave them their due in his directory:

'GLASS-GRINDERS

These Artists grind and polish Plate Glass after the Makers, and then silver it for Looking Glasses; or leave it transparent for Coaches, Chairs, &c.

Aldersey, Thomas	Glass-grinder and Cabinet-maker, Tooley-street, Southwark
Bazin	Chiswell-street, Moorfields
Bell, Richard & Co.	Bankside, Southwark
Bonick	Clerkenwell
Brightman	London Wall

[1] *The Plate-Glass-Book*, by 'A Glass-House Clerk', 3rd edition, 1760, page xi.
[2] Vol. I, under *Foliating*.

Eastlick	Hatton Garden
Hancox, Nicholas	Belton-street, opposite Brownlow-street, Long-acre
Huggit	Dowgate Hill
Lewis, Thomas	Little Queen-street, Lincoln's-inn-fields
Twaddell, William	Hanover-street, Long-acre
Unwin, Paul	St Mary Overy's, Southwark
Willis, William	Durham Yard, Moorfields

This Artist has polished the largest Glass that ever was made in England.

Wright, William	Crooked-lane, Cannon-street.'[1]

In 1835, Justus von Liebig, the German chemist, discovered that actual silver could be deposited in a thin film on glass. By about 1840 the process had become a commercial possibility, and true silvering quickly replaced the use of a tin and mercury amalgam. The newer method gives a more brilliant and hard-looking reflecting surface, but this is not always noticeable when old or dark-tinted glass is used. At the back of the plate the difference is quickly seen; tin and mercury silvering presents a granular metallic appearance, while the more modern process is finished with a protective coating of red lead (a brilliant orange-red in colour) or chocolate-brown paint. With exposure to damp the old surface tends to go grey, in patches often circular in shape, and glittering where tiny granules of metal have isolated themselves. The modern silver will tarnish completely where the air has reached it, and the granular appearance, alluded to, is not present.

[1] *The Universal Director*, 1763.

Silvered and painted wood carved in openwork with *putti*, owers and foliage; the cresting centred on a shield bearing the oat of arms of Gough of Old Fallings Hall and Perry Hall, taffordshire, granted in 1664. *c.* 1670. 5 ft. 9½ in. by 3 ft. 11 in. Victoria and Albert Museum)

Embroidered in coloured silks on silk, initialled 'M.C.' and with the date 1671 in the windows of the buildings in each pper corner. Probably intended for use on the toilet-table, but many examples have rings for suspension as well as struts for anding. The embroidered figure of Britannia (bottom, centre) an early appearance of this national emblem, who made her modern début on the copper halfpence of Charles II. According Samuel Pepys (*Diary,* 25th February, 1667), the King's favourite, rances Stewart, Duchess of Richmond and Lennox, was the nodel, but Britannia had been used much earlier during Roman mes, in the second century A.D. on coins of Hadrian and ntonius Pius. 1 ft. 8 in. by 1 ft. 4¾ in. (G. Noël Butler, Esq.)

Japanned wood decorated with oriental patterns, the glass ordered with four glazed panels of paper filigree work depicting irds, vases of flowers and floral meanders. *c.* 1685. 2 ft. 2 in. by ft. 6½ in. (Victoria and Albert Museum)

4. The frame veneered with 'oysters' of olivewood, and the cresting carved in openwork with scrolled foliage centred on a cipher. The design of this frame is similar to those in the engravings of Daniel Marot, and was in use in France and Holland as well as in England. This example could be claimed for all three countries. *c.* 1685. 5 ft. 7 in. by 3 ft. 1½ in. (Metropolitan Museum of Art, New York. Collection of Irwin Untermyer)

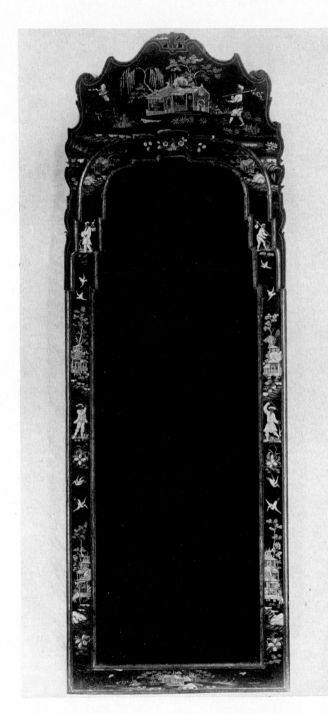

5. One of a pair. The glass in two sections; the frame with a shaped and pierced cresting and decorated with japanning in Oriental patterns. *c.* 1715. (Messrs Mallett & Sons, Ltd)

6. Cushion moulding veneered with pieces of imported Chinese 'Coromandel' or incised lacquer (known at the time as 'Bantam-work'), cut from a panel and used without any attempt to form a coherent pattern. *c.* 1685. 5 ft. by 3 ft. 3 in. (Victoria and Albert Museum)

Silver, embossed with *putti*, bunches and swags of fruit and flowers on riband against a background of foliate scrolls, the shaped pediment centred a cartouche with crossed C's and probably surmounted originally by a own. Presented with a table and two candlestands to King Charles II the City of London. *c.* 1670. 6 ft. 11 in. by 4 ft. 2 in. (Windsor Castle. eproduced by gracious permission of Her Majesty the Queen)

Embossed silver, the glass within gadroon and other mouldings and a rder of flowers and fruit, the shaped cresting centred on the Royal arms th supporters and the royal cypher beneath a crown. Presented with a ble and two candlestands to King William III by the City of London. 1697. 7 ft. 6 in. by 3 ft. 11½ in. (Windsor Castle. Reproduced by gracious rmission of Her Majesty the Queen)

The frame veneered with walnut and incorporating a barometer and a ermometer, the scale plate engraved: *John Patrick in the Old Baily Londini cit. c.* 1715. 3 ft. 5½ in. by 3 ft. 3¾ in. (Metropolitan Museum of Art, New rk. Collection of Irwin Untermyer)

10. The glass in two sections, within borders of cut and engraved glass. *c.* 1710. (Messrs Jas. A. Lewis & Son)

11. Bordered with panels of *verre églomisé* in gold on a blue ground, divided by narrow plates of engraved brass and surmounted by carved, silvered, wood cresting of strapwork and foliage centred on a helmeted female bust; the upper of the two glasses cut with formal design of three thistles. *c.* 1710. 7 ft. 7 in. by 2 ft. 10¾ in. (Victoria and Albert Museum)

2. Overmantel, with three bevelled arcaded plates bordered with panels of *verre églomisé* in blue and gold, overlaid with pierced and carved foliate strapwork at the cresting, base and angles. c. 1700. 5 ft. 6 in. wide. (Messrs Mallett & Son, Ltd)

3. Overmantel, with arched central glass, the blue glass borders secured and decorated with rosettes. c. 1700. 4 ft. 2 in. by 6 ft. 3 in. Hampton Court Palace. Reproduced by gracious permission of Her Majesty the Queen)

14. Overmantel, with shaped and diamonded glass borders, the two outer principal plates decorated with cutting in a formal floral pattern. *c.* 1710. About 4 ft. 6 in. wide. (Messrs Mallett & Son, Ltd)

15. Overmantel, bordered with panels of *verre églomisé* covered at the joins with navette-shaped pieces of engraved brass; the outer glasses decorated with cutting. *c.* 1710. (Messrs Mallet & Son, Ltd)

16. The three plates divided by strips of cut glass and the borders similarly decorated; the cresting surmounted by the coronet of a baron. *c.* 1710. (Messrs M. Harris & Sons)

17. The upper plate with cut decoration and an arched top, the diamonded border panels divided by narrow shaped and engraved brass plates; and the whole contained within painted and gilt mouldings. *c.* 1710. (Messrs A. Cook)

18. Two-plate pier-glass with diamonded borders, and scrolled cresting terminating in cut rosettes. *c.* 1710. (Messrs Jas. A. Lewis & Son)

19. Two-plate pier-glass bordered with panels of glass and with a shaped and arched cresting, in a gilt wood frame carved with gadrooning in the upper portion. *c.* 1715. (Messrs M. Harris & Sons)

(*Right*) The rectangular plate with two borders [of] glass having shaped brass plates concealing the [joi]ns; the elaborate cresting with shaped applied [gl]ass ornament centred on the arms and supporters [of] the 1st Duke of Devonshire. On it is scratched ['Jo]hn Gumley 1703'. (Chatsworth, Derbyshire)

21. (*Left*) The rectangular plates, bordered with cut glass divided by small shaped pieces of the same, and the cresting with the coronet and crest of the Earl of Nottingham. Supplied by Richard Robinson and Thomas Howcraft (*q.v.*) in 1711. (Burley-on-the-Hill, Rutland)

73

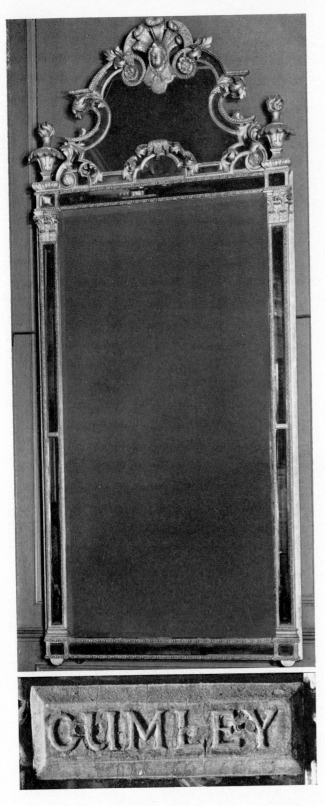

22. (*Left*) Pier-glass in a carved and gilt wood frame, the shaped cresting flanked by flaming vases and surmounted by a female head from which spring five feathers; the borders inset with strips of glass and headed at each side by corinthian capitals; the pilasters intersected by strips of gilt wood of which that on the left bears in raised letters the name of the maker: GUMLEY (See below). *c.* 1715. (Hampton Court Palace. Reproduced by gracious permission of Her Majesty the Queen)

22A. Gilt wood slip on the pier-glass of Fig. 22

23. (*Right*) Pier-glass with diamonded borders, the arched top with a gilt wood cresting carved with ribbed strapwork and curled acanthus leaves centred on a ribbed and foliate shell ornament. *c.* 1720. 6 ft. 10 in. by 2 ft. 9 in. (Messrs Sotheby & Co.)

24. Overmantel with three arcaded plates in a moulded walnut frame having a carved and gilt slip, the outer plates decorated with cutting which includes a crest. *c.* 1720. (Messrs Mallett & Son, Ltd)

25. Three-plate overmantel in a cushion moulded walnut frame, the outer glasses with cut ornament. *c.* 1720. About 6 ft. wide.
(Messrs M. Harris & Sons)

27. Pier-glass with shaped and diamonded borders, the base and cresting decorated with gilt gesso carved with scrolling foliage and with flowers and centred on shell ornaments; the corners of the cresting terminating in eagles' heads. Probably one of a pair of 'large Looking glass Sconces in carved and gold frames with double glass branches' supplied to John Mellor of Erthig by James Moore (*q.v.*) in 1720. (Erthig, Denbighshire)

26. Pier-glass with two plates, the frame ornamented with gilt gesso carved with interlaced strapwork and formal foliate ornament; the shaped cresting centred on a shell. *c.* 1720. 5 ft. 3 in. by 1 ft. 11 in. (Messrs R. F. Lock, Ltd)

28. Three-plate overmantel in a frame decorated with carved and gilt gesso. *c.* 1725. 1 ft. 7¾ in. by 4 ft. 2 in. (Messrs. John Keil, Ltd)

29. Pier-glass in a frame veneered with walnut within gilt mouldings and surmounted by a shaped cresting centred on a formal shell. c. 1725. (Messrs Mallett & Son, Ltd)

30. Pier-glass with glass borders, the shaped cresting decorated in gilt gesso with a pattern of strapwork and foliate scrolls centred on the coat of arms with crest, motto and coronet of the Duke of Norfolk. c. 1725. (Messrs M. Harris & Sons)

31. The glass with an arched top and contained in a narrow moulded gilt wood frame; with two swinging glass candle-arms hinged in shaped brass sockets. *c.* 1725. 2 ft. 7½ in. by 1 ft. 8 in. (Messrs Mallett & Son, Ltd)

32. Of similar shape to the preceding, but the moulded frame decorated in gilt gesso carved with a leaf pattern on a ground stamped with circular punch marks. *c.* 1725. 2 ft. 5 in. by 1 ft. 8 in. (Messrs John Keil, Ltd)

33. The shaped frame decorated in gilt gesso carved with scrolls and leafage on a punched ground, the cresting centred on a child's head in high relief above two conjoined wings. *c.* 1730. 2 ft. 10 in. by 1 ft. 8½ in. (J. V. Paterson, Esq.)

4. The moulded frame with shaped base and cresting decorated in gilt esso carved with scrolling leaves and husks; surmounted by three lumes, and fitted with swinging brass candle-arms in shaped sockets. 1730. (Messrs A. Cook)

5. The moulded frame with shaped base and cresting modelled in relief ith scrolls and centring on shells; decorated in gilt gesso carved in a attern of strapwork, scrolls and foliage on a ground of circular punch larks. c. 1730. (Messrs Mallett & Son, Ltd)

6. The moulded frame with shaped cresting, base and corners; decorated gilt gesso with foliage centred on shells, the ground stamped with rcular punch marks. c. 1730. 3 ft. 10 in. by 2 ft. 3 in. (Messrs R. F. ock, Ltd)

37. (*Left*) The moulded frame with shaped base and cresting decorated in gilt gesso carved with strapwork, flowers and scrolling leaves on a punched ground; the cresting surmounted by a shell between eagles' heads and with shells at the corners. *c.* 1730. 3 ft. 8 in. by 2 ft. (Messrs A. Cook)

38. (*Right*) Of similar general design to the preceding, the cresting centred on a group of five feathers between a broken swan-neck pediment and with rosettes at the outer corners. *c.* 1730. (Messrs M. Harris & Sons)

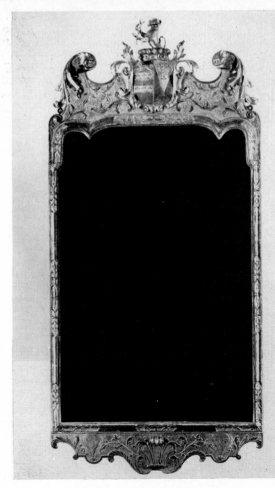

39. (*Left*) The upper of two plates decorated with simple cutting, the carved moulded frame inset with glass borders, and the base and cresting decorated in gilt gesso carved with foliage on a pitted ground; the cresting centred on a scallop shell before three feather-like ornaments between eagles' heads. *c.* 1725. 3 ft. 8 in. by 1 ft. 10 in. (Messrs Mallett & Son, Ltd)

40. (*Right*) The cresting with eagles' heads in high relief at the corners, and centred on a coat of arms and crest within foliate mantling. *c.* 1725. 3 ft. 5 in. by 1 ft. 10½ in. (Messrs Mallett & Son, Ltd)

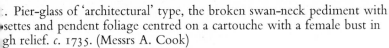

. Pier-glass of 'architectural' type, the broken swan-neck pediment with
rosettes and pendent foliage centred on a cartouche with a female bust in
high relief. *c.* 1735. (Messrs A. Cook)

. The upper part of the moulded frame modelled with eagles' heads in
bold relief, the cresting centred on a female head with feather head-dress
between a broken pediment decorated with foliage and flowers on a punched
ground. *c.* 1730. 3 ft. 7 in. by 1 ft. 11½ in. (Messrs Mallett & Son, Ltd)

. The moulded frame with shaped base, cresting and corners decorated
in gilt gesso carved with foliage on a punched ground; the cresting centred
in a pierced foliate shell. *c.* 1725. 4 ft. by 2 ft. 3 in. (Messrs Christie, Manson
and Woods, Ltd)

44. Overmantel in two parts: glass below and an oil-painting above; contained in a narrow frame decorated in gilt gesso carved with beading, scrolls and foliage. *c.* 1735. 5 ft. 2 in. by 4 ft. 9 in. (Messrs M. Harris & Sons)

45. The moulded frame veneered with walnut and with a carved gilt slip; both base and cresting shaped and similarly veneered, and the latter centred on a sunken carved and gilt shell. *c.* 1740. (Messrs Mallett & Son, Ltd)

46. Veneered with walnut and with a carved gilt slip, with a shaped base and cresting, the latter centred on a carved, pierced and gilt shell ornament, and the sides with carved pendent fruit, flowers and leaves. *c.* 1750. 4 ft. 10 in. by 2 ft. 1 in. (Victoria and Albert Museum)

47. Of very similar pattern to Plate 45. (Messrs Mallett & Son, Ltd)

48. (*Left*) Veneered with figured walnut and bordered with narrow carved and gilt mouldings, the broken swan-neck pediment having rosettes at the inner corners and centring on a basket of flowers and leaves. *c.* 1745. 5 ft. by 2 ft. 8¼ in. (Messrs John Keil, Ltd)

49. (*Right*) Veneered with walnut and with a shaped base and cresting, the latter with gilt applied foliated scroll carvings and a central eagle with outspread wings; the sides with carved and gilt pendent fruit and leaves. *c.* 1750. About 4 ft. by 2 ft. (Messrs Jas. A. Lewis & Son)

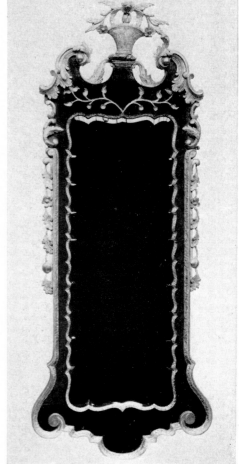

50. (*Left*) Of somewhat similar general pattern to Plate 49, but the finial in the form of a basket of flowers. *c.* 1750. 3 ft. 10 in. by 1 ft. 11 in. (Messrs Mallett & Son, Ltd)

51. (*Right*) Veneered with walnut and with carved gilt mouldings; pendent flowers, fruit and leaves in gilt wood at the sides; the cresting with incised and gilt formal leafage beneath a central basket of flowers flanked by foliate scrolls. *c.* 1750. 5 ft. 0½ in. by 2 ft. 10 in. (Victoria and Albert Museum)

83

52. The nearly rectangular plate within ribbon-and-rosette, chain-link and leaf mouldings and flanked by free-standing corinthian columns; a female mask in the lower frieze, and the whole surmounted by a broken swan-neck pediment centring on an urn draped with flowers. See note to Plate 53, below. *c.* 1730. (Messrs M. Harris & Sons)

53. Of somewhat similar design to the preceding, but lacking the mask in the lower frieze and with a rectangular plate; the upper frieze with an elaborate pierced pattern of scrolls and foliage and the straight broken pediment centred on a covered vase flanked by sprays of oak leaves. This and Plate 52 may be compared with a third looking-glass illustrated in F. Lenygon: *Furniture in England*, 1914 (p. 215, fig. 324), which exhibits features of both. All three are in the 'architectural' style with which the name of William Kent is associated. *c.* 1730. (Messrs M. Harris & Sons)

54. Of carved and gilt wood; the mouldings divided by a sanded ground and the low cresting centred on the coronet of the Prince of Wales with issuant feathers. Made for Frederick Louis, Prince of Wales (son of George II and father of George III), by Benjamin Goodison in 1732–3. (Hampton Court Palace. Reproduced by gracious permission of Her Majesty the Queen)

55. The rectangular plate bordered with bead-and-reel and leaf mouldings divided by sanding, the base and cresting decorated with gilt gesso carved with leaves on a punched ground, and the swan-neck pediment terminating in rosettes with pendent foliage and centred on a ribbed and fluted shell *c.* 1735. (Messrs Mallett & Son, Ltd)

6. One of a pair, the cresting centred on a mask of
[D]iana wearing a coronet embossed with a crescent and
[w]ith three plumes, flanked by hounds in pursuit of deer
[is]suing from foliage at either side; the remainder of the
[fr]ame composed of scrolling leaves and bulrushes centred
[on] shells at the base. *c.* 1735. 4 ft. 6 in. by 3 ft. 4 in.
(Messrs Sotheby & Co.)

7. The oval frame carved with guilloche moulding
[o]verlaid with foliage at intervals, surmounted by a standing
[o]wl from the beak of which depend swags of flowers
[an]d leaves, and at the base a child's head above wings
[th]rough which thread similar swags to those on the upper
[p]art. *c.* 1735. 5 ft. by 2 ft. 8 in. (Messrs Frank Partridge
[&] Sons, Ltd)

8. Oval, the guilloche moulding with entwined foliage
[ri]sing to a finial flanked by scrolls, and with the base
[tr]eated in a similar manner and centred on a boss. An
[an]onymous pen-and-ink and wash drawing in the
[V]ictoria and Albert Museum (reproduced in P. Ward-
[Ja]ckson: *English Furniture Designs of the 18th Century*,
[19]58, p. 36 and no. 35) shows a design for this looking-
[g]lass, together with another and a pier-table. *c.* 1740.
[A]bout 2 ft. 8 in. high. (Messrs A. Cook)

9. Oval, the plate bordered by an egg-and-dart moulding
[o]verlaid at each side with an acanthus leaf, the cresting
[i]n the form of a shield with a coat of arms beneath an
[E]arl's coronet flanked by pendent garlands of oak leaves
[an]d acorns bound and interlaced with ribands; the base
[c]entred on an elaborate shell. *c.* 1735. 5 ft. 9 in. by
[3] ft. 4 in. (Messrs Sotheby & Co.)

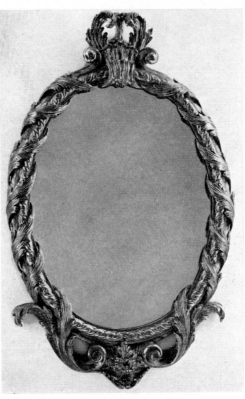

60. The sides with a male and female term, each wearing a head-dress, rising from scrolls and leafage; the base with a central group of birds on a nest of fruit, flanked by leaping hounds and resting on dolphins heads; the cresting composed of scrolls, foliage and baskets of fruit centred on a tasselled canopy beneath a leaf finial. Designed and carved by Matthias Lock in or about 1743. The original pen-and-ink and wash drawing by Lock for this frame is in the Victoria and Albert Museum, and is inscribe 'A Large Sconce for the Tapestrey Roome' together wit a note of its costs in time (138 days) and money. It is one of a group of seven drawings for furnishings in a mansion which has been identified recently as Hinton House, Hinton St George, Somerset; furnishings supplied probably when the second Earl Poulett inherited th estate in 1743. Lock's note of the cost of the frame totals £36 5s., of which the carving accounted for £34 10s. There i no note of a charge for gilding which may have been a separat matter altogether, or possibly may not have been carried out all. The partial bronzing is not older than the early 19th century. (See J. F. Hayward: *Furniture . . . by Matthias Lock f Hinton House . . .*, in the *Connoisseur*, December, 1960 (Vol. CXLVI, pp. 284–6).) 8 ft. 7 in. by 4 ft. 2 in. (Victoria and Albert Museum)

61. The sides with bacchante and satyr heads springing from scrolls with flowers and foliage; the base with a central ribbed shell shedding water and flanked by overturned vases of water; the cresting formed of a foliate scroll with an exotic bird at either side. From a design by Matthias Lock and perhaps made by him in about 1745.

The design for this looking-glass is Plate 4 in Lock's *Six Sconces*, published in 1744. The engraving is in reverse, left to right, to this frame. As a preparatory drawing would have been reversed similarly in normal practice, it is possible that this frame was made direct from the original drawing and perhaps prior to the publication of the print. Alternatively, it might have formed one of a pair of frames, one left-hand and the other right-hand. 3 ft. 10 in. by 2 ft. (Messrs A. Cook)

62. One of a pair, the sides with heads of river-gods above ridged scrolls and with fluted capitals above; the base with a central mask of Neptune wearing a crown and flanked by dolphins whose tails are threaded through the scrollwork; the curved cresting moulded and carved with lappets above flowers, foliage and a grotesque mask. From Elvaston Castle, Derby, seat of the Earls of Harrington, where there were some furnishings in the manner of Benjamin Goodison (q.v.), who may have been responsible also for these distinctive frames. c. 1740. 7 ft. 10 in. by 4 ft. 2 in. (Messrs Sotheby & Co.)

63. The plate with an arched top in a frame with rosette-and-ribbon and egg-and-dart mouldings; the top rising to a shaped column entwined with leaves and ribbons and containing a barometer; the base with a central head of Aeolus in relief, and the whole painted in cream on a black ground. c. 1740. 5 ft. 1 in. by 1 ft. 11 in. (Messrs Sotheby & Co.)

64. One of a pair, carved with shellwork, flowers and leaves, the cresting with a pierced shell terminating in a grotesque mask. c. 1745. 4 ft. 10 in. by 2 ft. 9 in. (Messrs Sotheby & Co.)

65. One of a pair, the moulded sides entwined with foliage and overlaid with shells, rising to a broken swan-neck pediment centred on a pierced and curled shell from which depends a ring with husks and leaves; the glasses divided by palms, and the base with a central ribbed shell. The original design by John Vardey is in the library of the Royal Institute of British Architects, London (reproduced by Ward-Jackson, op. cit., no. 43). The pair of glasses, with side-tables ensuite, were probably supplied to the Duke of Bolton in about 1750. (See A. Coleridge: John Vardy and the Hackwood Suite in the Connoisseur, January, 1962 (Vol. CXLIX, p. 12).) c. 1750. (Hackwood Park, Basingstoke)

6. (*Right*) The sides with scrolls, shellwork and acanthus
leaves; the cresting centred on the half-length figure of a
bearded and moustachioed Chinese wearing a tall conical hat
of leaves and holding in his left hand a parrot. *c.* 1745.
ft. 9 in. by 4 ft. 6 in. (Messrs Mallett & Son, Ltd)

67. (*Left*) One of a pair, the cresting centred on a basket of
flowers above a bacchante mask and flanked by exotic
birds; the sides with rams' heads, scrollwork and bunches
of rushes and fruit; the base with a mask of Bacchus.
Ensuite with a pair of commodes and formerly at Hampden
House, Buckinghamshire, seat of the Earl of Buckinghamshire.
c. 1755. 7 ft. 11 in. by 4 ft. 2 in. (Messrs Jas. A. Lewis &
Son)

68. The sides moulded, carved with leafage and tree branches, and rising to heads of Diana; the tall cresting framing a pendent group of dead game above a bow and quiver; the base with the head and fore-quarters of a running hound at each corner. *c.* 1755. 8 ft. 7 in. by 3 ft. 11 in. (Messrs M. Harris & Sons)

69. The frame carved with leaves and flowers, surmounted by a pierced scrollwork cresting framing two billing doves beneath an acanthus and cabochon finial; the whole partly gilt and partly painted grey. *c.* 1755. 6 ft. 8 in. by 3 ft. 9 in. (Metropolitan Museum of Art, New York. Collection of Irwin Untermyer)

70. With C-scrolls, leaves and columns with foliate capitals, the sides having intertwined branches of flowers and leaves. *c.* 1755. 4 ft. 6 in. by 2 ft. 6 in. (Messrs Mallett & Son, Ltd)

71. The design composed of similar elements to Plate 70, and with a more elaborate cresting of scrolls framing a flower. *c.* 1755. About 4 ft. 6 in. high. (Messrs Mallett & Son, Ltd)

72. The oval plate in a narrow border carved with foliage and flanked by pairs of open columns supporting pierced trefoil-topped canopies; the base of C-scrolls and leafage centred on rockwork with a balustrade; the cresting with a central figure of a seated Chinese beneath a Gothic arch which rises to a leafy canopy with a trefoil finial. *c.* 1755. 5 ft. 4 in. by 3 ft. 3 in. (Messrs Mallett & Son, Ltd)

73. Carved with scrolls, foliate branches and columns simulating masonry, the base centred on a pierced shell and the cresting in the form of curled leaves. *c.* 1755. 4 ft. 6 in. by 2 ft. 11 in. (Messrs John Keil, Ltd)

74. (*Left*) Carved with moulded columns, C-scrolls, foliage and flowering branches; the cresting centred on a pagoda-roofed pavilion supported on columns, flanked by pinnacled structures and with exotic birds at either outer corner. *c.* 1755. About 4 ft. 9 in. high. (Messrs M. Harris & Sons)

75. (*Right*) Of similar general pattern to the preceding; at the base a seated Chinese framed in C-scrolls; the tall cresting of foliage and flowers rising above a fountain and flanked by exotic birds. *c.* 1755. About 5 ft. high. (Private collection)

76. (*Left*) One of a pair the sides designed as moulded columns beside trees springing from the base through arches; the base with a central exotic bird; the tall cresting surmounted by a rustic pavilion with a domed top supported on tree-trunks; the corners with angular mouldings and falling water topped by vases of flowers; the plates divided vertically by columns with jars and falling water, and horizontally by a floral garland. *c.* 1760. 8 ft 3 in. by 3 ft. 11 in.

77. (*Right*) Double-columned sides entwined with flowers, and with rocks and falling water; the base of C-scrolls divided by shaped balusters and centred on a bunch of grapes with vine leaves; the cresting rising to a leaf ornament supported on three ribbed arches resting on fluted columns with a central fountain, and flanked by exotic birds at each corner. *c.* 1760. 7 ft. 7½ in. by 3 ft. (Plates 76 and 77: Brighton Royal Pavilion. Loaned by the trustees of the Earl of Chichester, Stanmer Park.)

. (*Right*) One of a set of four, with leafy scrolls and
[fl]owering branches; a seated squirrel at the base; in the
[ce]ntre a dead hare hanging beneath a coronet; surmounted
[b]y the figure of a seated man with a gun in his hand
[an]d wearing a leafy hat. The first of these four glasses
[w]as supplied to the Duke of Atholl for Dunkeld House
[in] 1761 and the estimate submitted on 28th September
[of] that year was for £50 for frame and glass, 'the
[fr]ame to be white and gold'. In 1763 three identical
[lo]oking-glasses were ordered for Blair Castle, the Duke's
[ot]her seat, and the bill for them was submitted by George
[C]ole. It totalled £168 for '3 very rich carved and gilt
[gl]ass frames . . . as before'. These glasses have been
[at]tributed for a long time to Thomas Chippendale,
[an]d the recent publication of the original estimate and
[C]ole's account prove that he was the supplier. It has
[be]en suggested, however, that they were actually
[de]signed and carved by Thomas Johnson, for they exhibit
[se]veral features common to his published work. (See
[A]nthony Coleridge: *Chippendale, The Director and some
Cabinet-makers at Blair Castle*, in the *Connoisseur*,
[D]ecember, 1960 (Vol. CXLVI, pp. 252–6); and Helena
[H]ayward: *Thomas Johnson and English Rococo*, 1964,
[p]p. 36–8.) *c.* 1763. 9 ft. 6 in. by 5 ft. 4 in. (Blair Castle,
[P]erthshire)

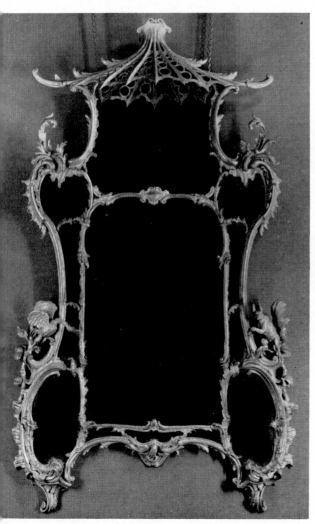

79. (*Left*) Moulded scrolling with leaves and shellwork, on the left an
exotic bird and on the right an enraged squirrel; the cresting in the form
of a pierced and ribbed canopy. *c.* 1755. (Messrs M. Harris & Sons)

80. Three-plate overmantel composed of scrolling and pierced shellwork with pendent flowers and leaves at either end; the cresting of acanthus leaves. *c.* 1755. 2 ft. 9 in. by 4 ft. 6 in. (Messrs R. F. Lock, Ltd)

81. Three-plate overmantel, the ends with columns simulating stonework and with foliate capitals, scrolls, leaves and shellwork; the top centred on a swan beneath a pagoda-shaped canopy of leaves; the plates divided by columns round which are entwined leafy branches. *c.* 1755. About 5 ft. wide. (Messrs Stair & Co., New York)

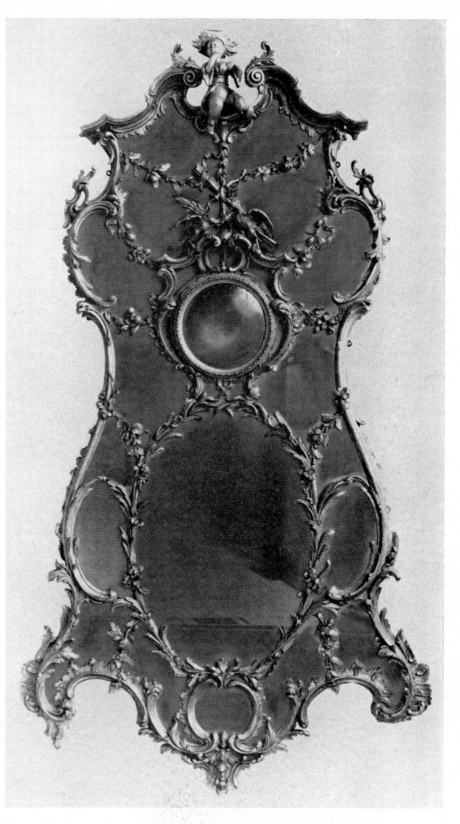

2. Gilt papier-mâché, at either side a seated figure below a pavilion, and the whole surmounted by a seated Chinese holding a parasol in his left hand and resting his right hand on a globe. *c.* 1760. 4 ft. 2 in. by 2 ft. 7 in. (Messrs Sotheby & Co.)

3. The sides in the form of moulded columns flanked by leafy branches springing from behind rustic buildings, and topped by scrolls, foliage and shellwork; the cresting of interlinked C-scrolls with falling water, surmounted by a pagoda-shaped canopy of leaves concealing a bell and with an encircling coronet above. *c.* 1755. 4 ft. 3½ in. by 2 ft. 2 in. (Messrs John Keil, Ltd)

4. One of a pair, the shaped frame of acanthus leaves and scrolls edged with shellwork; the plates divided by palm boughs and garlands of flowers; in the upper part a convex glass below a pair of birds and a bow and quiver; the shaped top surmounted by the figure of a Chinese youth carved in the round. *c.* 1760. 8 ft. 5 in. by 4 ft. 8 in. (Messrs Sotheby & Co.)

85. The branches at the sides supporting brackets for chinaware; the base with pierced fencing and a central leafy canopy supported on cluster-columns; the cresting with exotic birds at either corner and centred on the figure of a seated Chinese, leaning forward with his right hand raised, beneath a pierced canopy hung with bells. *c.* 1755. 5 ft. 10 in. by 3 ft. 8 in. (Messrs Mallett & Son, Ltd)

. The sides with moulded columns, scrolls
d leafy branches on which perch parrots;
e base with a sheep and a lamb grazing
d framed in C-scrolls; the tall cresting of
rolls and foliage surmounted by a leafy
nopy with a finial. *c.* 1755. 5 ft. 2 in. by
ft. 5 in. (Messrs A. Cook)

87. Leafage, C-scrolls, shellwork and leafless branches with the base centred on two ducks swimming beneath a brick arch flanked by balustrade and with hounds leaping from scrollwork at either corner; on the left a monkey playing a violin with a bird above, and on the right a monkey blowing a pipe with a marmoset above; beneath the shaped tall cresting a fox, and at the upper corners two squirrels; the plates divided by moulded columns entwined with leaves and by garlands of wheat ears. c. 1755. 7 ft. 8 in. by 4 ft. 6 in. (Messrs Frank Partridge & Sons, Ltd)

. The oval plate framed in egg-and-dart moulding and shellwork
erlaid with scrolling and foliage, and with an exotic bird at each
e; the cresting with a central flower beneath leaves and flanked by
untains. From a design by Thomas Johnson in his untitled
blication of 1758, plate 10, centre left-hand, and plate 55 in his
e Hundred and Fifty New Designs, 1761. The lower brackets shown in
engravings are lacking, but may have been omitted originally by
maker. *c.* 1760. 3 ft. 7 in. by 2 ft. 4 in. (Messrs John Keil, Ltd)

89. Oval, the sides with a female head on the left and
a male head on the right, both wearing fanciful hats;
the base terminating in a vigorously carved leafy
scroll; the cresting surmounted by a large dragon
with outstretched wings. From a design by Thomas
Johnson, on plate 8, centre left, in the 1758 publication,
and plate 23 in that of 1761. *c.* 1760. 5 ft. 3 in. by
3 ft. (Messrs A. Cook)

90. Carved with scrolling, foliage and shellwork, the sides with bulrushes; the base fitted with metal candle-arms issuing from rockwork; the cresting flanked by exotic birds. This looking-glass exactly matches a pair sold at the dispersal of the Bernal collection in 1855, one being then purchased by the Museum of Ornamental Art, later the Victoria and Albert Museum. The two were catalogued separately, lots 4149 and 4150, as being 'by Chippendale'. This glass is possibly the one (lot 4150) not purchased by the museum but sold at the same time for £40. It was originally surmounted by a vase of flowers, and there were tall leaves at each side behind the birds. (See *Catalogue of English Furniture and Woodwork*, V and A., 1931, vol. iv, p. 48 and plate 32.) *c.* 1765. 5 ft. 9 in. by 4 ft. (Messrs Frank Partridge & Sons, Ltd)

91. Somewhat similar to the preceding. This looking-glass was also perhaps in the Bernal collection, where a pair was sold separately as lots 4143 and 4144; the former being bought by the old Museum of Ornamental Art and the latter realising £38. In the *Catalogue* (*op. cit.*) of the Victoria and Albert Museum Department of Woodwork this and the preceding looking-glass were confused with 'two very large Oval Glasses' supplied to the Duke of Portland in 1766 (see page 149). At one time this frame had candle-holders springing from the rockwork at the base. *c.* 1765. 6 ft. 3 in. by 3 ft. 7 in. (Messrs A. Cook)

2. The moulded column and scroll sides flanked by tree trunks springing from rockwork; the base with a central acanthus motif framed
by C-scrolls and flanked by waterfalls emerging from shellwork; the cresting centred on a Chinese with drooping moustachios seated
beneath a canopy of palm leaves. *c.* 1765. 6 ft. 6 in. by 3 ft. 2 in. (Messrs Sotheby & Co.)

3. The sides formed of columns and scrolls with intertwining leafy branches; the base in the form of a fanciful balustrade with short
curved flights of steps at the corners; the cresting with a Chinese pavilion having a pagoda-shaped roof of leaves. *c.* 1760. 7 ft. 4 in. by
2 ft. 11 in. (Messrs Sotheby & Co.)

94. The sides with moulded columns and leafy branches on which perch exotic birds; the elongated cresting with a leafy-roofed pavilion resting on leafy C-scrolls with a central balustrade and rockwork. From a design by Matthias Lock and Henry Copland; plate 6, left, in their *New Book of Ornaments*, first published in 1752. *c.* 1755. (Messrs Mallett & Son, Ltd)

95. Composed of moulded C-scrolls with shellwork and leaves; the cresting rising to a pointed finial of scrolls flanked at the corners by exotic birds. *c.* 1760. About 7 ft 6 in. high (Messrs R. F. Lock, Ltd)

One of a pair, framed in C-scrolls with
shellwork and cascading water, and moulded
columns with foliate capitals; at each side
a large exotic bird with raised head; the
cresting centred on a turbanned oriental
youth seated in a pavilion with an imbricated
roof and flanked by palm branches springing
from rocks. From a design by Thomas
Chippendale, closely following plate
CLXIII in the first (1754) edition of the
Director, but deviating in having a
seated figure instead of a standing one in
the upper pavilion. In the same house are
other looking-glasses, girandoles and
bookcases, all of which follow designs in the
Director and it is presumed they came from
the St Martin's Lane workshops.
Unfortunately, there is no documentary
evidence to confirm what is at present only a
probability. *c.* 1755. (Crichel House, Dorset)

103

97. One of a pair, with C-scrolls and moulded columns flanked by leafy branches rising from rock-work and tiered balustrades; the cresting centred on an oriental musician in a pavilion with a leafy roof and tall leaf finial. From a design in Ince and Mayhew's *Universal System of Household Furniture* (1759–62), plate LXXX, left, which has been followed faithfully except for the cresting. Ince's design shows a fanciful arrangement of knotted ropes and tassels above a scroll with shellwork, and the present Oriental is a pleasing variant on the part of the maker. In the same vein he has added the small squirrels at the top corners. *c.* 1760. 9 ft. 6 in. by 4 ft. 7 in. (Metropolitan Museum of Art, New York, Morris Loeb Gift, 1955)

98, 99. Pair of pier-glasses. These combine in their extremely fanciful design both European and Oriental elements in such profusion that description is scarcely possible. They epitomise the English eighteenth century's careless confusion of East and West that forms *Chinoiserie*; a style that delights many and disgusts others. While the acceptance of their design is a matter of choice, it must be agreed that the carving of these frames is a *tour-de-force*. c. 1760. 11 ft. 1 in. by 3 ft. 2 in. (Victoria and Albert Museum)

100. One of a pair, the heart-shaped central plate framed in foliage and flowers; the base of conjoined foliate scrolls flanked by intertwined scrolling leafage; the cresting rising above a pierced shell to an anthemion finial. *c.* 1770. 7 ft. by 3 ft. 2 in. (Messrs Vernay, New York)

101. Formed of crossed oak branches bearing leaves and acorns and with ribands at the intersections; two further branches rising to form the tall cresting. *c.* 1770. (Messrs A. Cook)

102. (*Left*) Oval, framed in pierced shellwork overlaid with leaves and intertwined with flowers and fruit; the cresting with a pierced shell framed in C-scrolls. *c.* 1770. About 4 ft. 3 in. high. (Private collection)

103. (*Right*) Oval, composed of foliate scrolls and shellwork, and with garlands at each side; the base centred on figures of a sheep and a goat framed in C-scrolls. *c.* 1770. About 4 ft. high. (Private collection)

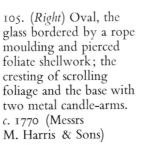

104. (*Left*) Oval, the border of C-scrolls and pierced shellwork, with leaves rising at each side from the base; the cresting a pierced shell ornament. *c.* 1770. 3 ft. 8 in. by 2 ft. 3 in. (Messrs John Keil, Ltd)

105. (*Right*) Oval, the glass bordered by a rope moulding and pierced foliate shellwork; the cresting of scrolling foliage and the base with two metal candle-arms. *c.* 1770 (Messrs M. Harris & Sons)

106. (*Left*) Shaped oval, the frame of scrolls, foliage and shellwork rising to a tall leaf ornament held between C-scrolls framing a bouquet of flowers and leaves, which is repeated at the base. *c.* 1770. (Messrs A. Cook)

107. (*Right*) Oval, framed in a foliate gadroon moulding, set within an elaborate and delicate composition of scrolls, leafy branches, bouquets and shellwork. *c.* 1770. (Messrs M. Harris & Sons)

108. (*Left*) Oval, the inner moulding bordered with pendent garlands of fruit and flowers; the cresting of leafy scrolls and shellwork with a central pierced shell ornament. *c.* 1770. (Messrs A. Cook)

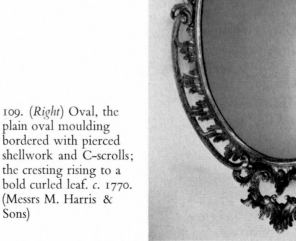

109. (*Right*) Oval, the plain oval moulding bordered with pierced shellwork and C-scrolls; the cresting rising to a bold curled leaf. *c.* 1770. (Messrs M. Harris & Sons)

110. (*Left*) Oval, bordered with pierced shellwork and leafy scrolls; the cresting in the form of an acanthus leaf. *c.* 1770. 3 ft. 7½ in. by 2 ft. 3½ in. (Messrs A. Cook)

111. (*Right*) Oval, with plain and foliate scrolls and pierced shellwork; the cresting an acanthus leaf rising above a shell ornament framed in C-scrolls. *c.* 1770. (Messrs A. Cook)

112. (*Left*) Oval, leafy branches crossing at the base, and rising to an intertwined cresting with flowers at the intersections. *c.* 1770. (Messrs A. Cook)

113. (*Right*) Oval, with leafy branches crossed at the base and rising to a horse-shoe shaped crest, with flowers at the intersection and at the lower part of the frame. *c.* 1770. (Messrs A. Cook)

114. Oval, framed in leafy scrolls with shellwork, rocks and cascading water, and with garlands at the sides; the tall cresting of scrolls surmounted by a tree flanked with exotic birds. *c.* 1770. (Messrs A. Cook)

115. Oval, framed in a moulding carved with ribbon-and-rosette and other ornament, at each side a winged mermaid with entwined tail; the cresting composed of cornucopias spilling flowers, and with ribbed scrolling and foliage rising to an acanthus leaf. Resembling a glass supplied by Samuel Norman (*q.v.*) and James Whittle to the Duke of Bedford, and ascribed to the same makers. *c.* 1760. 7 ft. 2 in. by 3 ft. 2 in. (Victoria and Albert Museum. Photograph: Frank Partridge & Sons, Ltd)

116. One of a pair having C-scrolls bordered with pierced shellwork, and garlands at each side; the cresting of egg-and-dart moulding surmounted by a ribbed shell and flanked at the corners by eagles. *c.* 1760. (Rudding Park, Harrogate)

117. In a gilt pinewood and papier-mâché frame with C-scrolls, foliage and shellwork rising to a finial in the form of a basket of flowers; the plates divided by moulded columns with foliate capitals, and by scrolls and a garland. *c.* 1765. 7 ft. by 3 ft. 7 in. (Messrs John Keil, Ltd)

118, 119. A pair of girandoles modelled with C-scrolls with shellwork, flowers at each side, and the tops with pavilions and seated figures of squirrels. *c*. 1760. (Messrs Mallett & Son, Ltd)

120. (*Left*) One of a pair of sconces with cut decoration, and blue-glass shaped strips radiating from the brass candle-arms. *c*. 1700. 3 ft. by 1 ft. 4 in. (Metropolitan Museum of Art, New York. Collection of Irwin Untermyer)

121. (*Right*) One of a set of four sconces made to fit in the corners of a room; each cut with a star at the top and fitted with a shaped candle-arm modelled with the head and neck of a swan. *c*. 1715. 2 ft. 8½ in. by 3¾ in. (Metropolitan Museum of Art, New York. Collection of Irwin Untermyer)

122. Overmantel, composed of leafy scrolls, shellwork and cascading water (sometimes termed 'icicles') and with two candle-holders on each side; the lower part with figures of sheep beneath ruined masonry arches and with trees rising from rockwork; the cresting surmounted by a bunch of flowers above an exotic bird and flanked by monkeys, one playing a pipe and the other with a bird on its left paw. c. 1760. 4 ft. 7 in. by 5 ft. 8½ in. overall. (Messrs Phillips of Hitchin, Ltd)

123. One of a pair of girandoles formed of moulded columns and C-scrolls, surmounted by a bird and with metal candle-arms springing from each side. c. 1760. (Messrs M. Harris & Sons)

124. One of a pair of girandoles formed of an obelisk and a tree on which is perched a parrot, and with leafy scrolls rising to an acanthus finial; fitted with two metal candle-arms at the base. c. 1760. (Messrs M. Harris & Sons)

125. Overmantel, the central oval glass flanked by
shaped sections within a framing of moulded scrolls
and foliage with shellwork and floral ornament;
candle-arms at the base, and an exotic bird at each
upper corner. c. 1765. 4 ft. 4 in. by 5 ft. 5 in.
(Messrs Frank Partridge & Sons, Ltd)

126. Overmantel, the frame of fluted columns,
C-scrolls and foliage, with exotic birds on
rockwork; the cresting carved with Ganymede
and the Eagle. The latter appear in the same
pose as the finial of an overmantel, which
bears no other resemblance to this one, in Thomas
Johnson's volume of designs of 1758, plate 36,
and his *One Hundred and Fifty New Designs*, 1761,
plate 19. c. 1760. 4 ft. 2 in. by 4 ft. 4 in. (Victoria
and Albert Museum)

127. Overmantel, the elaborate gilt wood frame composed of C-scrolls and shellwork set against a background of trellis and with leaves and flowers at each side; the shaped glass in the lower part flanked by exotic birds facing each other in threatening attitudes; the upper section containing an oil-painting of a winter scene with skaters on a river with buildings and ruins in the background, signed by George Smith, of Chichester, and dated 1761. Smith (1714–76) probably painted it especially to fit the frame. *c.* 1760. 7 ft. 10 in. by 4 ft. 1 in. (Messrs Jas. A. Lewis & Son)

128. Overmantel, with an oval central glass framed in foliage and shaped borders within C-scrolls and garlands; a painting above, and the whole surmounted by a basket of flowers. The design for this overmantel and chimneypiece by John Linnell (q.v.) is in the Victoria and Albert Museum. (Reproduced by Edwards and Jourdain: *Georgian Cabinet-Makers*, 1955, fig. 165.) c. 1760. (Osterley Park, Middlesex)

129. Oval, composed of C-scrolls and shellwork with uprising foliage at each side; the openwork base and cresting with leaf and scroll ornaments. c. 1770. 4 ft. 4½ in. by 2 ft. 5 in. (Messrs Christie, Manson & Woods, Ltd)

130. One of a pair of girandoles with column scrolls and shellwork; each surmounted by an exotic bird perched on a curved balustrade. c. 1760. (Messrs M. Harris & Sons)

131. Oval, papier-mâché, the plate bordered with husk-and-bead ornament; with leafy scrolls at either side rising to a cresting with a pierced leafy canopy above a female mask; the base fitted with two metal candle-arms. c. 1770. (Messrs A. Cook)

132. Overmantel, the central glass painted in China with pheasants, paeonies and roses; the English frame of scrolling foliage with pierced shellwork and icicles; the plates divided by moulded columns with capitals from which rise leafy plants; the cresting in the form of a balustrade with a pagoda-shaped canopy of leaves. c. 1765. 2 ft. 4 in. by 4 ft. 2 in. (Messrs Mallett & Son, Ltd)

133, 134. A pair of Chinese paintings of birds and flowers executed on looking-glass; the English frames of scrolls and foliage surmounted by figures of exotic birds. c. 1765. Each 3 ft. 11½ in. by ft. 0¾ in. (Messrs Christie, Manson & Woods, Ltd)

135. Gothic pattern, with moulded column joined by cusps and leafy branches; the cresting with foliate arches flanking a pierce shell ornament supported on scrolls. *c.* 1765. (Messrs Mallet & Son, Ltd)

136. Gothic pattern, th sides of cusp and rosett moulding beside columns with foliate capitals separated by trellis; the base of arches and columns above a row of arches and trefoils; the crestin in the form of a large cusp overlaid with ribands, topped by a trefoil and flanked by pierced steeples. *c.* 1765 4 ft. 8 in. by 2 ft. 6 in. (Messrs Mallett & Son Ltd)

137. Overmantel, of mixed Gothic and rococo design; the leafy scrolls, shellwork, and branches of flowers interspersed with cusps and pointed arches. *c.* 1765. About 4 ft. 6 in. wide. (Messrs A. Cook)

138. Gothic pattern, the frame painted in black and with gilding. In the *Strawberry Hills Accounts* is the following: '1755 Sept. 20. d. Hallet for black frames to Gothic glasses £13 0 0', and in Horace Walpole's *Description* of Strawberry Hill, 1774, is: 'For the Great Parlour: On each side of the window . . . re cardtables . . . and over each, looking-glass in a gothic frame of black and gold, designed by Mr Walpole.' The one illustrated contains portrait of George Walpole, third Earl of Orford, copied by J. G. Eckardt from a miniature by Liotard. It was lot 60 on the 18th day of the dispersal at Strawberry Hill in 1842, when it realised £13 2s. 6d. 5 ft. 9 in. by 2 ft. 9 in. (Wolterton Hall, Norfolk)

139. Mahogany, carved and pierced in an elaborate pattern of military and musical trophies, rosettes, and an eagle with outspread wings at the base; the cresting of scrolling leaves centred on a shell with trellis background, flanked by eagles at the corners. This type of flat, although lively, carving is ascribed usually to Irish craftsmen. *c.* 1765. (Messrs Jas. A. Lewis & Son)

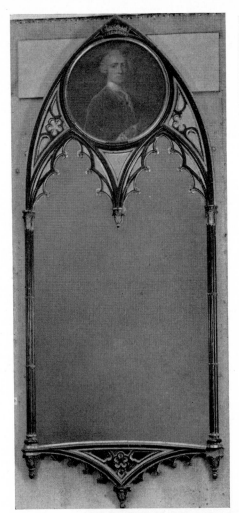

140. Oval, the moulded frame carved with palmettes and beading; the base and cresting of scrolling leaves with paterae. The original invoice for this looking-glass records that it was supplied in 1774 by Chippendale and Haig for the sum of £16 16s. (See A. Coleridge: *Chippendale, Interior-Decorator and House-Furnisher*, in *Apollo*, April 1963, p. 295.) (Paxton House, Berwick-on-Tweed)

141. Plain pinewood, carved with scrolls, pierced shellwork and flowers; the elaborate cresting similarly composed and surmounted by an eagle with outstretched wings. Probably made in Ireland (see Plate 139). *c.* 1760. (Messrs R. F. Lock, Ltd)

142, 143. The Glass Drawing Room at Northumberland House, Charing Cross, London, Designed by Robert Adam, 1770–74. The photographs show the room *in situ* before it was demolished in 1874 when the present Northumberland Avenue was built. The walls of the room were lined with glass back-painted in red and appearing like polished panels of an imaginary stone that is a cross between porphyry and aventurine, and mounted with gilt metal ornaments; pier-glasses and an overmantel were decorated similarly with applied gilt metal. The original water-colour drawings by Adam are in the Soane Museum, and a part of one is reproduced in J. Lees-Milne, *The Age of Adam*, 1947, fig. 2. Some portions of the actual room have been preserved and are exhibited in the Victoria and Albert Museum, to which they were presented by the late Dr W. L. Hildburgh. (Photographs: Victoria and Albert Museum)

144. Pier-glass with classical ornament, the sides with female terms and pendent husks; the cresting of scrolled foliage and paterae surmounted by an anthemion. The original design for this looking-glass by Robert Adam, which is in the dining-room at Syon, is in the Soane Museum. *c.* 1765. (Syon House, Middlesex)

145. Pier-glass, the sides in the form of palm trees and the plates divided by branches of the same; the cresting centred on a shield painted with the coat of arms of the first Lord Scarsdale flanked by supporters and surmounted by a coronet and by a massive group of leaves. Probably designed and supplied by John Linnell. *c.* 1765. (Kedleston Hall, Derbyshire)

146. Overmantel, the centre plate with an arched top; the columns ornamented with palmettes, husks, and rams' heads, and the ends surmounted by covered vases with draped and suspended laurel garlands.
 A feature of this looking-glass is that the end columns are thinner from back to front at their bases than at their tops, so that it will lean forward slightly when fixed in position. This difference is a matter of two inches. *c.* 1775. 3 ft. 8 in. by 6 ft. (Messrs A. Cook)

147. (*Left*) Oval, in a moulded frame with bead and gadroon carving; the cresting in the form of a fluted bowl of wheat ears raised on leaves and from which depend flowering branches. *c.* 1775. 4 ft. by 2 ft. 2 in. (Messrs Stair & Company, New York)

148. (*Right*) Oval, somewhat similar to the preceding, but with a more elaborate and distinguished cresting. *c.* 1775. 4 ft. 5 in. by 1 ft. 9 in. (Private collection)

149. (*Left*) Oval, with bead, fluting and egg-and-dart mouldings, the sides with chains of husks depending from rams' heads; the base with crossed palm boughs and the cresting surmounted by a covered vase with flame finial. *c.* 1775. 5 ft. 9 in. by 2 ft. 8 in. (Messrs Sotheby & Co.)

150. (*Right*) Oval, with bead, fluting and gadroon mouldings, the base with a central patera, husks, scrolled leaves and an anthemion; the cresting with a covered vase and chains of husks. *c.* 1775. (Messrs Stair & Company, New York)

151. Pier-glass designed by Robert Adam for the Tapestry Room, Croome Court, Worcestershire. Made by Ince and Mayhew. The original account to the Earl of Coventry reads: 'Oct. 5, 1769. To Mayhew & Ince. A large Architect Pier Frame, fluted, richly carv'd with shell on top, festoons and drops of double husks down the sides, goates head at bottom gilt in the very best Double Burnish'd Gold £35.' (See J. Parker: *Croome Court, the Architecture and Furniture*, in *Bulletin of the Met. Mus. of Art*, Vol. XVIII (1959–60), pp. 79–95.) *c.* 1770. 8 ft. 9 in. by 5 ft 6 in. (Metropolitan Museum of Art, New York. Gift of the Samuel H. Kress Foundation, 1958)

152. Gilt papier-mâché and pinewood, the glasses divided by reed-and ribbon moulding and by garlands of berried leaves; the cresting centred on a shell from which depend chains of husks; the base with a central covered vase framed in leafy scrolls and flanked by pierced ornament. *c.* 1770. 7 ft. 8 in. by 4 ft. 8 in. (Victoria and Albert Museum)

153. One of a pair, the shield-shaped plates each surmounted by figures of otters and with a central covered vase with oak leaf and acorn swags gathered by paterae and ribbons.

In the Duchess's Drawing Room at Stowe, Buckinghamshire, was a pair of looking-glasses included in the 40-day auction sale of 1848. On the second day, August 16th, lot 247 reads: 'A pair of vase-shaped pier-glasses, with otters on the frames, carved with foliage in festoons'. It is unfortunate that no size is given in the catalogue, but the room is 50 feet by 35 feet by 18 feet in height. These present glasses tally with the brief description, and would certainly not have looked out of proportion on the walls 'hung with rich crimson damask'.

The south front of the mansion, in which was situated the Duchess's Drawing Room, was rebuilt between 1775 and 1790, perhaps to the design of Thomas Pitt, Lord Camelford. Pitt was a keen amateur architect and in that capacity earned the esteem of Horace Walpole, for whom he designed the 'ornaments' of the Gallery and the Chapel at Strawberry Hill. Alternatively, the work at Stowe has been attributed to J. B. Borra. Either of these men might have designed the looking-glasses, but it is uncertain whether they were made especially for Stowe or came from elsewhere. c. 1780. 9 ft. 6 in. by 4 ft. 4 in. (Messrs Sotheby & Co.)

154. One of a set of six girandoles designed by Robert Adam. These were probably made by John Linnell, but with some divergences from Adam's original design which is in the Soane Museum. c. 1770. 7 ft. 6 in. by 5 ft. (Osterley Park, Middlesex)

155. The plate bordered with husks which divide it from an outer framing of glass, contained within bead and egg-and-dart mouldings; the cresting of leafy scrolls supporting an anthemion; the base with three candle-arms fitted with glass nozzles and grease-pans. *c.* 1775. 5 ft. 1 in. by 2 ft. 8 in. (Messrs Mallett & Son, Ltd)

156. Overmantel, the fluted canopy hung with oriental gongs and with dragons at the corners. The cluster-column mouldings at the sides replace the original members which were removed in 1851 and are believed to have been of palm-tree design. The whole looking-glass and frame cost the sum of £1,608 11s. when it was supplied. (H. D. Roberts: *History of the Royal Pavilion*, 1939, pp. 134–5.) *c.* 1820. 12 ft. 5 in. by 8 ft. 4½ in. (excluding canopy). (Brighton Royal Pavilion, by courtesy of the Committee)

157. (*Left*) Oval, with a border of faceted and fluted blue and clear silvered glass cubes. Irish. *c.* 1785. (Messrs Jas. A. Lewis & Son)

158. (*Right*) Oval, with a border of panels of *verre églomisé* within carved mouldings and with the joins masked by oval paterae. *c.* 1780. 3 ft. 10 in. by 2 ft. 11 in. (Messrs Mallett & Son, Ltd)

159. (*Left*) The rectangular plate flanked by corinthian columns, and surmounted by a frieze inset with a panel of *verre églomisé. c.* 1810. 3 ft. 4 in. by 1 ft. 10½ in. (Messrs Mallett & Son, Ltd)

160. (*Right*) The side columns overlaid with leaves at intervals, the shallow frieze with a moulded leaf pattern and overhung with a row of balls; the top surmounted by a plinth bearing a black-painted eagle with a chain of balls depending from its beak and linked to flanking paterae. *c.* 1815. (Messrs Mallett & Son, Ltd)

161. Convex glass with a circular reeded slip in an octagonal frame; the moulding carved with leaves and at the outer edges as a sunburst. *c.* 1815. (Messrs Jas. A. Lewis & Son)

162. Convex glass with an ebonised slip within a cavetto moulding set with balls and with a ribbon-and-reed edge; the base in the form of crossed palm boughs; the cresting with an eagle upon conjoined snakes; the whole suspended from ribands with an elaborate bow. *c.* 1815. 4 ft. 5 in. by 2 ft. 8 in. (Messrs A. Cook)

163. Convex glass with ebonised slip and cavetto set with balls; the top surmounted by an eagle with outstretched wings holding in its beak two chains from which hang balls at each side are two candle-arms with metal nozzles and glass pans and buttons. Labelled: 'Thomas Fentham 136 Strand, Manufacturers of Looking Glasses.' *c.* 1820. 2 ft. 3 in. (Messrs Phillips, Son & Neale, Ltd)

164. Convex glass with ebonised reeded slip, the moulded frame with leaf and bead-and-bobbin carving and with stars set between; flanked by two pairs of candle arms; the base of curled leaves the cresting with an eagle set on foliage encircled by a laurel wreath. *c.* 1820. (Messrs Jas. A. Lewis & Son)

Appendix 1. Parliamentary Proceedings Relating to the Cast Glass Company

THE following is an extract from the *Journal of the House of Commons*, volume XXXIV, 26th November, 1772, to 15th September, 1774, pages 64, 149–50, 163, 239 and 263.

Anno 13   George III   25th January, 1773

'A Petition of the honourable *Charles Fitzroy*, the honourable *Robert Digby*, *Peregrine Cust*, *Thomas Dundas*, *John Mackay*, *Philip Affleck*, *Henry Dagge*, *James Bourdieu*, *James Mowbray*, *Angus Mackay*, *Henry Hastings*, *Ranald Macdonald*, and *Samuel Chollett*, was presented to the House, and read: Setting forth, That the Petitioners, having great reason to believe that considerable Improvements may be made in the Glass Manufactory of this Country, and particularly in the Manufactory of large Plates, have formed themselves into a Society, for the Purpose of establishing a Work of that Kind, under the Name of "The *British* Cast Plate Glass Manufacturers"; and have already engaged several Persons of Skill and Knowledge in the Business; but, in regard to the great Expence which will attend the Undertaking, the Petitioners are advised, they cannot establish nor carry on the same, to a sufficient Extent, nor on a permanent Foundation, or with Safety, unless formed into a Company, and authorised by Parliament to make proper Rules, Ordinances, and Bye Laws, and are invested with such Powers, Rights, and Privileges, as may tend to the effectual establishing, conducting, and improving, the said Manufactory: And therefore praying, That Leave may be given to bring in a Bill for incorporating the Petitioners and their Successors, under the Name of "The Governor and Company of *British* Cast Plate Glass Manufacturers"; and for vesting them with such Powers and Authorities, for the better and more effectual establishing, directing, managing, and carrying on, the said Manufactory, in such Manner as in the said Bill is intended to be set forth, or as the Parliament shall think meet and convenient.

'*Ordered*, That the said Petition be referred to the Consideration of a Committee: And that they do examine, and state to the House, the Matter of Fact contained in the said Petition:

'And it is referred to Mr *Mackworth*, Sir *Charles Bunbury*, &c.; And they are to meet To-morrow Morning, at Nine of the Clock, in the Speaker's Chamber, and have Power to send for Persons, Papers, and Records.

24th February, 1773

'Mr Mackworth reported from the Committee which had been appointed to hear the Petition, as follows:

'It appeared to your Committee, by the Evidence of Mr Philip Besnard, that he had been engaged in the Manufacture of making Plate Glass 15 Years; and he said, He had studied the Art 25 Years, and had made Plates of Glass in Picardy and Burgundy, Ten Feet high and Six Feet wide, or 130 by 90 Inches, French Measure; and that these Glasses were made by casting them upon a Table; that since his coming to England, which is about 18 months, he had made Enquiry after English Plate Glass, and the largest he has seen, was 40 by 36 Inches; has heard of larger being made but could never get the Sight of any: That the English Glass is blown in general, and that it is impossible to blow Plates of Glass of the first Magnitude; that there are all Necessaries in England for making of Glass, except Barilla, and that it is practicable to make Glass Plates of the first Magnitude equally as well in England as in France, there being no want of Materials; that there is a great Difference between Blown and Cast Glass, for Three Reasons; the Cast Glass may be made larger, clearer, and cheaper, and that the Risque is greater in blowing than casting; the Works and Apparatus for casting Glass, both with Respect to the Buildings, Furnaces, Cooling Ovens, Copper Tables for casting, and other Matters, are formed upon a very different Construction from the Glass Houses in England: The whole Apparatus upon an extensive Plan, with every Necessary that is requisite, may be estimated at £50,000, but the necessary Buildings for the First Establishment will cost about £12,000; and with the Materials, and Expences attending the Work, may amount to £25,000, before any Return of Money can be made from the Manufactory: That he is engaged to carry this Plan into Execution with a Set of Gentlemen.—And being asked, Why none of the largest Size Plate Glass was made in England? he said, Because they don't understand the Art; that all the Buildings, and every Necessary to carry on the Trade to its utmost extent, is included in the Estimate of £50,000.—In France they pay no Duty on Glass or Barilla, because they would encourage the Trade, but when imported into England, it pays a Duty of 80 or 90 per Cent. and he knows Glass has been imported into England to a large Amount, £3,000 being paid for Commission in a Year. And he further said, That the Glass Manufactory in Venice, is now very trifling; but the French cannot cast it fast enough for their Consumption, it being exported over all the World. In England he has heard that a Duty is paid, of about 9 Shillings per Cent. on the gross Materials used, but he thinks Plate Glass may be made cheaper in England than in France, because Fuel is much cheaper here, and the French Manufactory is established in a bad Situation for Fuel—that the French cast Plates, from Ten Guineas to 100 Guineas Value per Plate; the Price of Glass runs from 5s. to £4 per Foot: And being asked, Whether the best Glass that he has seen in France, was better than the best he has seen in England? he answered, That he had seen a great Number of English Glasses, but that the French Glass was the best, because they are more clear, more white, and transparent.

'It appeared by the evidence of Mr James Christie, Auctioneer, that a great Quantity of French Plate Glass goes through his Hands every Year; that the largest English Plate Glass he has ever seen does not exceed, in Length, the Width of the French Glasses, they measuring from 65 to 68 Inches in Width, and from 114 to 118 Inches in Length; he sold Three Pair of large French Plates for £2,500. He further said, That he had seen a large Glass, at a House belonging to the Proprietor of the Glass Manufactory at Vauxhall, which was shewn him as a Prodigy, and he could not help smiling, when he considered its Size in a comparative View with the Glass he had seen of Foreign make; it appeared also to him very faulty: And he lamented much that such large Sums of Money should go Abroad (amounting, as he believed, from 60 to £100,000 per Annum) for Foreign Glass, which might be saved at Home, could a similar Manufactory to that in France be established in England. The Duty on French Glass is 75 per Cent. with 8d. per Pound or thereabouts on Importation, but he believes not One Third of the Quantity that is imported pays Duty, being in general smuggled; and a Kind of trading Company has been formed here for that Purpose: He thinks, if this Manufactory is brought to Perfection, it will be from 500 to £1,000 per Ann. out of his Pocket, which he now gains by Commission on the Sale of Foreign Glass; and the Witness supposed that Foreign Glass, to the Value of £10,000 went through his Hands last Year, and 20,000 through many of the Warehouses; and he imagines, from the Number of Glasses that he has seen of Foreign make, that they must amount to nearly the Sum before-mentioned; he has known One Pair of Glasses sell for £1,000. The Witness said, He never saw any Glass manufactured in England, but always understood that it was made by blowing only, which he thinks may be as good in that Mode as if it was Cast, but that it is not possible to go to so large a Size. In France he thinks he saw 1,000 People employed in a Manufactory in the various Branches, as grinding, polishing, &c. and they seemed to be happy in their Employment. He said, The Proprietor of the Manufactory of Glass at Vauxhall had been applied to for large Plate Glass, but he refused to engage in that Branch, he having a sufficient Trade in the less Sizes; and said, He did not choose to run so great a Risque, for the Duty was very high. He further said, That he did not know, by Inspection, the Difference between cast and blown Glass; that he has seen French Glass as perfect as possible, and in proportion to the Number, more perfect than the English; that the large English Glass is apt to wave: And the Witness said, He had often mentioned the

Utility that a Manufactory of large Plate Glass would be of to this Country, to the Right Honourable Charles Townshend, from the great Quantities of Foreign Glass being imported; and he was given to understand, if such an Undertaking was set on Foot, that every possible Encouragement would be given by Parliament and Administration, as a great National Object. He did not remember to have sold English Glass exceeding 30 Inches wide and 60 long—the Tariff for Glass of the largest Dimension is only $48\frac{1}{2}$ by 60; and he thinks, if Plate Glass could be made upon more moderate Terms, a large Quantity of such Plates would be exported to the East Indies and elsewhere, though at present he knows of no Exportation from England, while a very considerable one is carried on from France.

'It appeared by the evidence of Mr John Mayo, a Cabinet Maker and Worker of Plate Glass, that he apprehends it to be all blown, as he never heard of its being cast in England; has known French Glass bought by Commission for Exportation; and he does not doubt but great Quantities would be exported from England, if made as cheap and perfect as in France, and should suppose it may be made cheaper: And the Witness said, He has been informed, the King of France is concerned in the Glass Manufactory, and is at a great Expence therein; and also, that the Trade is there carried on by a large Company; that he has imported a great deal of French Glass, upon Account of the Size; and, notwithstanding the heavy Duty thereupon, it comes less expensive than the English; that he applied at Vauxhall for Plate Glass, but could get none made there, on Account of the Size he wanted, as there were none so large, and they did not chuse to make them; the largest English Plates of Glass he ever saw, were about 36 Inches by 72.

'It appeared by the Evidence of Mr Bowles, that he made a great Quantity of Plate Glass, the largest Size, 82 by 48; and that he could make larger Plates, but there is no Sale for them; he has a Glass in his Possession of 99 or 100 Inches long, and 40 Inches wide, which was formerly cast; but has now no Apparatus for casting Glass, it having been long since destroyed: He does not recollect the Price of those he made of the larger Sort, except one Glass, 60 by 40, sold for £37 10s. in the rough; he believes French Glass is cheaper.

'It appeared by the Evidence of Mr Dickson,[1] that at Mr Cookson's Manufactory for Plate Glass, the largest Size made is 84 by 52 Inches, which he believes were cast. This Manufactory has been carried on for 30 Years; and said, He could be supplied with Plates of that Size from thence; but as there is no call for them (the French underselling us) very few had been made, and he could not tell the Price: That he could not export them, because there was no Demand: And being asked, What he would sell a Glass of 84 Inches by 52 for? he said, For any Price, but they are rough.

'Mr Quinton informed your Committee, that he had made very few Plate Glasses as yet,

[1] James Dixon was London agent to John Cookson, of a well-known Newcastle family connected with glass manufacture. The glasshouse at South Shields was opened in 1738 by John Cookson in partnership with Thomas Jefferys. They had London warehouses at London Bridge and Blackfriars Stairs (1740), and in Fleet Street (1756). Francis Buckley: *Glasshouses on the Tyne in the Eighteenth Century*, in *Journal of the Society of Glass Technology*, Vol. X, 1926, pages 33–4, and for the subsequent history see *The Newcastle Chronicle*, 12th May, 1854, page 6 ('The Workshops of the Tyne. No II, Messrs. Swinburne & Co's Glass-works').

the largest Size was 84 by 38 Inches, but that he had never sold One; that he could cast large Glass Plates, but not in the Manner they do in France.

'A Member[1] present informed your Committee, that he had received a Letter lately, wherein he was informed, that at a Manufactory he was concerned in, they had just begun to blow Plate Glass; and he had made One Plate 65 by 38 Inches.'

2nd March, 1773

'*Ordered*, That Leave be given to bring in a Bill to incorporate certain Persons . . . for the purpose of establishing One or more Glass Manufactories . . . for the casting of large Plate Glass.'

1st April, 1773

'Bill read the third time, and "*Ordered*, that Mr *Mackworth* do carry the Bill to the Lords, and desire their Concurrence".'

6th April, 1773

'The Lords have agreed to the Bill . . . without any Amendment.'

7th April, 1773

'Royal Assent given.'

[1] Probably Sir Matthew Ridley, member of Parliament for Newcastle-upon-Tyne, who was concerned in a glasshouse at Howden-Pans, Wallsend. This was converted to plate-glass manufacture in 1772, but suffered damage from fire in the following year. It is presumed to have ceased making plate-glass shortly after 1773. (Buckley, ibid., page 35.)

Appendix 2. *Verre Églomisé* and Chinese 'Mirror Pictures'

ENGRAVING on gold under glass, known as *verre églomisé*, can be considered an art in itself, and it was used at various times as part of the embellishment of looking-glasses. For that reason, some words about the process, its history and its applications, are not out of place here.

The descriptive term *verre églomisé* was applied to the work at some time after a Paris art-dealer and auctioneer, Jean-Baptiste Glomy, who died in 1786, popularised placing a border of black and gold painted on the inside of the protective glass, round prints and drawings.[1] When set off in this manner, they became known in France as *églomisées* and in Italy as *agglomizzati*. For want of a better name it has become usual to employ it to describe all types and periods of engraved gold work executed behind glass, but as it did not become current until the nineteenth century it has been denounced as an anachronism. This is true enough, but there is no other suitable term at present by which it might be replaced.

As pointed out by the late W. B. Honey,[2] details of the method were recorded by Cennino Cennini in his manuscript *Il libro dell' Arte*, written at Padua in the late fourteenth century, where it is stated that the selected piece of glass is to be coated on one side with glair (white of egg and water) on which is laid thick gold leaf. When this has dried hard, the pattern is inscribed carefully with a fine needle, the background is scraped away, and the whole painted in a colour to enhance the engraved lines and the remaining gold.

[1] Glomy is remembered also for contributing additions to the first *Catalogue Raisonné* of Rembrandt's etchings; that of Gersaint, published in Paris in 1751 and in London in the following year.

[2] W. B. Honey: *Gold Engraving Under Glass*, in *The Connoisseur*, December, 1933 (Vol. XCII, pp. 372–81).

Examples dating from classical times have survived, fragments having been found embedded in the mortar used in the walls of the Roman catacombs. The fourteenth century saw a revival of the art in Italy, and gradually it spread to other countries in Europe; its use was confined at first mainly to the ornamentation of religious articles like portable altars, but in time it appeared on secular pieces. A novel method of employing it to decorate drinking-glasses, both goblets and beakers, was practised in Bohemia during the second quarter of the eighteenth century, examples of which are known as *Zwischengoldgläser*. In this, a glass decorated externally with gold engraving was given a protective outer coat by fitting to it accurately another glass. So carefully was the work done that the method of making is scarcely discernible.

In the late eighteenth century a Dutchman named Zeuner painted unusual and decorative pictures, principally of views in Holland and England but seascapes are known, in which the skies were painted in grey to contrast with the engraved silver and gold of the other portions. The artist exhibited at London in 1778,[1] and there are examples of his work, including a view of Sadler's Wells Theatre, London, signed but undated, in the Victoria and Albert Museum. Others are in English private collections, in the Rijksmuseum, Amsterdam, and elsewhere on the Continent. Dated examples range from 1775 until about 1800.[2]

Panels of *verre églomisé* were used to make decorative borders for looking-glasses during the years 1680 to 1700, and they are found ornamenting the tops of the glasses fashionable during the Regency. In the first instance they were usually patterned with geometrical designs in gold on red, blue, green or black backgrounds, and on rare occasions a monogram or coat of arms was added. Early nineteenth-century glasses of rectangular shape were surmounted often by a panel decorated either entirely in engraved gold or else in colours framed in gold.

Chinese mirror-paintings, in their effect resembling the work of Zeuner, albeit much more colourful, can be considered as an offshoot of the art of *verre églomisé*, although, strictly speaking, the term is reserved for those employing gold and silver leaf in the manner of the Italians and Romans and their eighteenth-century Dutch follower. Polychrome work of the Chinese type was mentioned by Robert Hooke in 1674:

'Saw a curious way of back-painting on the backside of a looking glasse at Mr Bartue chamber in pump court 2p. of stairs high';[3]
and in France in 1676 there is an entry in the *Compte des Bâtiments* of Louis XIV: '*le peintre Boulongne ayant peint des glaces de miroir dans un "appartement des attiques" à Versailles.*'[4]

[1] At the Society of Artists of Great Britain: 'A Drawing of a Landscape in Metals on Glass', and 'A Ditto, it's Companion'. The address of the painter (whose surname only appears in the catalogue, and elsewhere) was 28, Haymarket.

[2] Thieme-Becker: *Allgemeines Lexicon der bildenen Künstler*, 37 vols, Leipzig, 1907–50.
[3] *The Diary of Robert Hooke*, ed. H. W. Robinson and W. Adams, 1935, page 113.
[4] Havard: *op. cit.*, Vol. II, page 993.

One of the numerous Jesuit missionaries in China, Father Castiglione (1688–1766), was in high favour with the Court at Pekin under the Emperors Yung Chêng and Ch'ien Lung. He was famous there for his skill as an artist, and it has been suggested that he was responsible for the introduction there of this unusual form of painting at which the Chinese quickly grew adept.[1] By 1745, at least one painting of this type had reached the West and was described by a Frenchman, but they did not arrive in numbers for a further five or ten years. The art was apparently practised also in France at this time, for the *Annonces Affiches et Avis Divers* of 5th February, 1755, mentions '*sieur Vispré de Besancon qu'il faudrait faire remonter l'invention de ses fraiches peintures executées sur des parties de miroir dont le tain a été préablement enlevé*'. Soon afterwards, in the *Année littéraire* for 1758 and 1762 and the *Mercure* of June, 1759, the reinvention was ascribed to a painter named Jouffroy, of Dijon. He was said to have executed in backpainting portraits of Marie Leczinska and the Comtesse de Brionne, and an allegorical group of Louis XV as Jupiter with Minerva and Victory.[2]

It is apposite to record here another use for the term 'Back-Painting', mentioned above, which was employed sometimes for the process of making what are termed 'Glass Pictures'. These were made by sticking a mezzotint or other engraving face downwards on a sheet of glass with the aid of varnish, and when dry, removing the surplus paper at the back with friction until only the printed lines remained. Colouring was then applied, also at the back, and in spite of the perfunctory manner in which this was done the effect is not unpleasing. These pictures are well-known as decorations in their own right, but they were used sometimes to ornament the friezes of early nineteenth-century looking-glasses.

Although the Chinese attempted to make looking-glass, their efforts were unsuccessful. A Swedish ship's chaplain, Peter Osbeck, who was at Canton in 1751, noted: 'The mirrour-makers have some little pitiful looking-glasses. I was told of a glass-house in *Canton*, but never had an opportunity of going to see it. It is said, the importation of glass from *Europe* is forbidden. However, the *Europeans* often bring glass with them, and get roses and other flowers painted on them, as the *Chinese* are pretty skilful that way.'[3]

The process employed by the Chinese in making the pictures was for the artist to take a sheet of looking-glass, draw his design on the back of the silvering, and then scrape away carefully the places where he wanted to paint. This he did usually with gum-based colours, but sometimes oils were used. The finished pictures show a wide variety of subjects, both figures

[1] See M. Jourdain and R. Soame Jenyns: *Chinese Export Art of the Eighteenth Century*, 1950, in which Chapter III is entitled 'Paintings on Glass', and George R. Loehr: *Missionary Artists at the Manchu Court*, in *Transactions of the Oriental Ceramic Society, 1962–3*, vol. 34, page 51, which deals principally with enamel-painting, but includes important information about Castiglione and others.

[2] Ibid.

[3] Pehr Osbeck: *Dagbok öfwer Ostindisk Resa*, Stockholm, 1757. A German translation was published at Rostock in 1765, and from this an English version was made by J. R. Forster, 2 vols., London, 1771. The latter was entitled *A Voyage to China and the East Indies*, and included also *A Voyage to Suratte, China, &c.*, by Olaf Toreen, Chaplain of the *Gothic Lion*. The quotation is from vol. I, p. 233. The present writer acknowledges the kindness of Mr R. J. Charleston, Keeper of the Department of Ceramics, Victoria and Albert Museum, in drawing his attention to this work.

and landscapes, many of them of purely Chinese design, but as the century progressed these were supplanted by an increasing proportion copied from Western engravings taken East for this purpose. A mid-eighteenth-century traveller commented: 'Their painters would acquit themselves very well, if they knew how to shade. You meet with very fine drawings painted on paper and glass; and likewise the very worst.'[1]

While the majority were on sheets of normal plate looking-glass, mostly with the edges bevelled, a few examples were executed on glass made by the 'crown' process: recognisable unmistakably by its thinness and the misshapen furrowed surface. Some of these latter paintings date from about 1755–60, and it is assumed that the glass for them came from Europe together with the more usual plate glass.

Many of the pictures reaching Europe came in Chinese-made frames of hardwood or lacquered softwood, but many were framed or reframed when they arrived. For this purpose, some of the most skilful craftsmen were employed, and their facility for creating pseudo-Oriental fantasies in gilded wood were given full vein. The makers and designers of the frames remain anonymous, but the results of their work are among the most felicitous expressions of eighteenth-century *Chinoiserie*: an aligning of East and West that surely gives the lie to Rudyard Kipling's 'never the twain shall meet'.

[1] Olaf Toreen, ibid., vol. II, p. 245.

Appendix 3. Papier-Mâché and Other Compositions

THE introduction of papier-mâché (literally, chewed or mashed paper) to England is obscure, but as early as 1672 its use for ornamenting picture-frames 'and other Curious Movables' was advocated by the Hon. Robert Boyle.[1] Its use in the seventeenth century is uncertain, but it certainly became more popular as the eighteenth century advanced, and grew to a sizeable industry in Victorian times.[2] One of the first to be connected with it was William Wilton, father of the sculptor and Royal Academician, Joseph Wilton (1722–1803).

John Thomas Smith, a Keeper of Prints and Drawings in the British Museum, wrote a gossipy book entitled *Nollekens and His Times*,[3] in which the life of the sculptor, in whose studio he had once worked, was the occasion for providing the reader with much additional biographical material irrelevant to the main subject but often of great interest. The second volume of the work contained a number of biographies of contemporaries of Joseph Nollekens, and that of Joseph Wilton, R.A., opens as follows:

'Joseph Wilton was born in London, July 16th, 1722. He was the son of a plasterer, who, by a vast increase of income, arising principally from a manufactory, in imitation of that in France, which he established for making the papier-mâché ornaments for chimney-pieces, and

[1] In an essay entitled *Of Man's great Ignorance of the Uses of Natural Things*.
[2] See J. Toller: *Papier-mâché in Great Britain and America*, 1962.
[3] The book was first published in 1828, and a second edition with additional material followed a year later. The latter was reprinted with copious notes by Wilfred Whitten (2 volumes, 1920), and forms the most useful modern edition.

frames for looking-glasses, was enabled to rebuild his premises on the south-west corner of Hedge-lane, Charing-cross; at the same time enlarging his workshops on the west side of Edward-street, Cavendish-square, where his ornamental works were carried on: in which hundreds of people, including children as well as grown persons, were for several years constantly employed.

'These premises, for many years after Wilton left them, were occupied by a glass-manufacturer of the name of Hancock, for whom Dr Johnson wrote a shop-bill.'[1]

Smith relates also how Mrs Nollekens was in Covent Garden in the company of Mrs Elizabeth Carter, the essayist and scholar, talking to a man named Twigg, a fruiterer who had once been cook 'at the Shakespeare Tavern, and knew all the wits and eccentrics of his early days'. After some questions had been answered satisfactorily, Mrs Nollekens asked him about a house in James Street where her father's old friend, James Grignon, the engraver, resided. Twigg replied: ' "No. 27 . . . I recollect the old house when it was a shop inhabited by two old Frenchwomen, who came over here to chew paper for the *papier-mâché* people." Mrs Nollekens: "Ridiculous! I think Mr Nollekens once told me that the elder Wilton, Lady Chambers's grandfather, was the person who employed people from France to work in the *papier-mâché* manufactory, which he established in Edward-street Cavendish-square." Twigg: "I can assure you, Ma'am, these women bought the paper-cuttings from the stationers and bookbinders, and produced it in that way, in order to keep it a secret, before they used our machine for mashing it." '[2]

The immediate French origin of papier-mâché seems confirmed by its name, although it is known that it was used commonly in Persia and elsewhere in the East at an earlier date. In England, it became very popular after Henry Clay of Birmingham took out a patent in 1772 from which he proceeded to amass a fortune estimated at £80,000, but it was certainly in use here for a number of purposes well before that date. It is said that William Wilton's variety went under the name of 'Fibrous Slab', and was composed of plaster and vegetable matter: hay, straw, nettles, treebark, etc., and it has been reported also that this material was used at the time for ornamenting frames and 'chair knees'.[3] No examples of it in the latter role appear to have survived, but a well-known set of chairs with knee ornaments of gilded pewter makes it seem possible that papier-mâché might also have been so employed.[4]

Dossie gives 'The method of preparing and moulding papier-mâché, and whole paper, for the forming of boxes, frames, festoons, &c.', and explains that it can be made from paper pulped and mixed with glue, gum arabic or isinglass, the resulting composition being put into

[1] Hedge Lane is the present Whitcomb Street by the National Gallery and Edward Street disappeared when Langham Place was formed. The 'glass-manufacturer of the name of Hancock' was Colebron Hancock, a cutter of useful and decorative glass other than looking-glass plates, and there is no record of Samuel Johnson having penned anything on his behalf or even of his having known him.
[2] Whitten, *op. cit.*, vol. 1, page 172.
[3] J. Toller, *op. cit.*
[4] Examples are in the Untermyer collection, New York, and the Victoria and Albert Museum, London.

prepared moulds of plaster or wood that have been heavily greased. Alternatively, simple articles could be made by building them up, also in moulds, from sheets of paper pasted one on top of another 'with a paste of a thin consistence, made by boiling flower and water for a long time, and adding afterwards about two ounces of common size to a pound of the paste'.[1]

An early reference to papier-mâché occurs in that mine of contemporary information, the letters of Mrs Delany. Writing to her sister, Mrs Anne Dewes, on 17th December, 1749, she records that she is on a visit to London and adds: '. . . I took a chair to do business; went in the first place to Mr Dufour's, the famous man for paper ornaments like stucco, bespoke a rose for the top of her Grace of Portland's dressing-room . . .'[2] From the tone of the sentence it appears that the material was no novelty to her and that it must have been on the market for some years to have made the seller 'famous'. One of his trade-cards, somewhat later in date than the foregoing episode, has been preserved, and reads: 'Duffour CARVER & GILDER. Original Maker of Papie Mâchie at the Golden Head, in Berwick Street, Soho. London.', written elegantly within a rococo framework ornamented with birds and surmounted by a female bust.[3]

Either the rose was put aside for a period or it had been used and was discarded, because four years later, on 21st December, 1753, Mrs Delany wrote to her sister from Bulstrode, where she was residing with her friend, the Duchess of Portland: 'We are all in disorder at present. The Duchess's dressing-room all unfurnished to have a *papier-mâchée* ceiling put up; but we hope it will be finished to-morrow, and then we shall be very busy in setting it in order again.' A week later the situation was unchanged: 'I have not been able for a fortnight past to send you any of the Duchess's fine seals, for her dressing-room is pulled to pieces, filled with scaffolds, and the ceiling ornamenting with papier-mâchée, and all the seals are in the great table, which cannot be got at till I write next.'[4]

A few years after the above was written, in September, 1756, Dr Richard Pococke visited Lord Foley's mansion, Witley Court, in Worcestershire. He recorded: 'The whole of the church above and on the sides is richly adorn'd with papier maché gilt in imitation of the finest carvings.'[5]

Later again, in February, 1762, a foreign visitor to the capital for the coronation of George III visited the home of Mrs Stanley, daughter of Sir Hans Sloane. He wrote in his dairy: '. . . she lives with her two unmarried daughters in a very well furnished house . . . To the ceilings of the rooms, which are papered, and which have been evenly painted, decorations of *papier maché* have been added, and I must confess I should never have taken it for what it really is.'[6] No doubt many a looking-glass frame was also not 'taken for what it really is', which may explain a scarcity of contemporary evidence about them.

[1] *Handmaid to the Arts*, 1758, vol. II, page 361 *et seq.* (1764, II, p. 397).

[2] *The Autobiography and Correspondence of Mary Granville, Mrs Delany*, edited by Lady Llanover, 6 vols., 1861–2, vol. II, page 532.

[3] Repr. Heal: *London Furniture Makers, 1660–1840*, 1953, page 51.

[4] *Op. cit.,* vol. III, pages 260 and 262.

[5] *Travels Through England*, 2 vols., Camden Society, 1888–9. Vol. II, p. 230.

[6] Count Frederick Kielmansegge: *Diary of a Journey to England, 1761–2*, 1902, pages 249–51.

Thomas Johnson, 'Carver, Teacher of Drawing and Modelling and author of a Book of designs for Chimney pieces and other ornaments; and of several other pieces',[1] issued a book of designs in 1758. It was published without a title-page, and page one bears instead a dedication and the legend 'Sold by T. Johnson Carver. At the Golden Boy, in Grafton Street, St. Ann's Westminster . . . 1758'. The lettering is 'within a frame on which Britannia is seated, while, above, a winged genius sets fire with a torch to a fragment of *rocaille* and a scroll inscribed French Paper Machee'.[2] This does not allude to the einflammability (or otherwise) of the material, but to the Anti-Gallican Association.

This body was formed in 1745 'to oppose the insidious arts of the French Nation'. It awarded prizes of money for the making of lace lappets and needlework ruffles and for the weaving of brocades, and a medal was given for whale-catching. At a meeting in January, 1754, 'five guineas were ordered to an honest, industrious old couple, who are greatly distressed by the loss of their cows, from the distemper amongst the horned cattle'.[3] The Association is remembered less for its apparently circumspect actions than for its splendid badge with the motto 'For Our Country', which was engraved by Robert Hancock and used on pieces of Battersea enamel.[4] Stephen Theodore Janssen, owner of that short-lived enterprise, was a Grand-President of the Anti-Gallicans.

The Grand-President in 1758 was Lord Blakeney, who had defied the troops of Louis XV at Minorca, and to whom Thomas Johnson's book was dedicated. In the Dedicatory Epistle the author dubs himself 'an Englishman . . . who possesses a truly Anti-Gallic Spirit', and doubtless one who feared injury to his livelihood as a wood-carver from an extended use of the French substitute.

Mortimer's *Universal Director* of 1763 listed a few men who were makers of papier mâché, and later directories give increasing numbers of them. The following were noted by Mortimer:

Babel, Peter   Designer and Modeller, Long Acre, near James-Street—One of the first Improvers of Papier Mache Ornaments for Ceilings, Chimney-pieces, Picture-frames, &c. an invention of modern date, imported by us from France, and now brought to great perfection.

Middleton, Charles   Modeller, Chaser in Bronze and Papier Mâché Manufacturer in Tottenham-court-road, near Windmill-street.

Shrouder, James   Modeller and Papier Mâché Manufacturer, Great Marlborough-street, Carnaby-market.

An engraving of a frame in the rococo style with dragons, a Chinaman's head, a small pagoda and two billing doves, lettered 'G. Bickham according to Act of Parliament, P. Babel

---

[1] Thomas Mortimer: *The Universal Director*, 1763.
[2] P. Ward-Jackson: *English Furniture Designs of the Eighteenth Century*, 1958, page 48.
[3] *Gentleman's Magazine*, vol. 24, page 44.
[4] The badge has been found printed on some Bow porcelain plates, see Cyril Cook: *Supplement to the Life and Work of Robert Hancock*, 1955, item 125. It was used also, but painted by hand, on mid-eighteenth century Chinese 'export' porcelain.

Invent. 1752', is reproduced by Ward-Jackson.[1] He remarks that it 'is stated in the imprint to be after P. Babel, the French artist, but it bears little resemblance to his work'. Under these circumstances, it is possible that the inspirer was Peter Babel, the maker of papier-mâché noted above, rather than the Parisian designer, Pierre-Edmé Babel. The etching probably came from one of two booklets: *A New Book of Ornaments, from Babel* or *A New Book of China Ornaments from Babel*, which were announced as having been published in the *Gentleman's Magazine* for March and April, 1753, respectively.[2] Both were issued by Vivares, and the price of the first, given at 1s., indicated that it was a half-dozen or less pages in content.

From about the middle of the eighteenth century papier-mâché mounted on a shaped wood backing was used sometimes for completely framing a looking-glass,[3] but often it is found to comprise only a portion of the ornament. From the front, when the entire frame is gilded, the imitation and the carved wood are indistinguishable from one another. Only by careful inspection of the back can the difference sometimes be detected, and a liberal application of yellow ochre, the normal finish for all frames, can prove very misleading.

The use of substitutes for carving other than papier-mâché is an old practice. Salmon gives precise instructions for taking moulds from a carved frame and then casting from them by using a mixture as follows:

'Make a Glew-water stronger than any Size, yet something weaker than Joyners melted Glew: mix Whiting in fine pouder therewith, till it is as thick as Paste or Dough; knead it very well, wrapping it up in a double Cloth; in which it may lye and get heat from the Fire; for you are not to let it grow cold, for then it will harden, and so be made unfit for Use.'

He advises making the casts in sections, each of which is to be glued into place on the newly-made unadorned frame. 'Let it alone to dry for 5 or 6 days; after which you may safely lay your white Ground, which you may Paint, Varnish, Japan, Gild in Oil, or Burnish, as the Nature of your Work requires'.[4]

The use of such compositions for decorating the frames of looking-glasses is found occasionally on examples dating from the last quarter of the eighteenth century onwards. Many of the fanciful designs of Robert Adam, with their swags of delicate husks and other details, were impossible to realise in wood, and were made from putty-like materials that were moulded, set on wires and dried rock-hard. Adam also used lead for similar features, and an example of this is to be seen in the part of the Glass Drawing Room from Northumberland House, Strand, exhibited at the Victoria and Albert Museum (Plates 142 and 143). Here, the joins between the panels of looking-glass and painted glass with which the walls are panelled are concealed by slender strips of gilded lead formed to the design of the architect.

[1] *Op. cit.* page 40 and fig. 70.   [2] Vol. XXIII, pages 150 and 203.
[3] *The Reading Mercury and Oxford Gazette*, 5th December, 1768, printed the advertisement of an auction sale at Hall Grove, Bagshot, Surrey, which included 'Pier and other Glasses in Papier Machee Frames'. Quoted by R.W. Symonds: *Furniture-Making in 17th and 18th Century England*, 1955, page 158.
[4] *Polygraphice*, 1701, chapter XX, page 911.

Appendix 4. Speculum, or Steel

SPECULUM is a silvery-white alloy that takes a high polish, and does not tarnish quickly under normal circumstances. Confusingly, it is referred to sometimes as Steel, but its only likeness to steel is in sharing the same name. William Salmon wrote:

'The reason why these Metalick Glasses are called *Steel Glasses*, is not from their being made of Steel, for there is no Steel in them; but *from the very great Hardness of their Temper and Composition*, equalising that of Steel; these being extremely hard, white, and not very brittle, and therefore the more easily polished, and made admirably fine.'[1]

It was used widely for looking-glasses of small size before the general introduction of glass for the purpose, but, because of its great weight in proportion to its size, it was confined to small pieces. It continued to be employed for scientific purposes, such as for the reflecting mirrors of telescopes and microscopes, and for those popular eighteenth-century contrivances, burning-glasses.

Salmon gives the following formula, which is recommended as being 'fit for flat Looking-Glasses:

'Refined Rose Copper lb. iij. melt it, then add of fine Tin lb. ix. as soon as they are melted, add red Tartar calcined xviij. white Arsenick vj. Nitre iij. keep these in a melting heat for 3 or 4 hours, that the salts may evaporate; then cast it into the Moulds.'

A further receipt from the same source gives different ingredients and method, adding 'by which means it will be so hard as not to be touched with a File, and as good as Steel for our Intended Uses'.

Polygraphice, 1701, page 853.

143

Polishing of the cast plate was not dissimilar to that of glass, and if the work was done well the final result was little different. Salmon gives a final note of warning:

'*If these Glasses are sullied or made dull with the Air or any thick Vapour*, you must clear them by rubbing, not with Woollen or Linnen, but with a piece of Deer or Goats Skin, wiping it in an oblique line.'

Surviving flat plates of old Speculum are not many in number, and it is not possible to say whether any of them were made in this country or imported from the Continent. Well-known examples include a heavy piece, six pounds in weight, of rough shape but measuring 10 by 12 inches overall, exhibited at Cotehele House, Cornwall. It is in a frame of the late seventeenth century which has been given an inner 'slip' mount of roughly oval shape to hide the irregular outline of the piece of metal. At the back the uneven surface reveals the rough casting which must have been equally apparent on the front before it was polished, and patches of pink colouring are indicative that copper was used in its composition.[1]

[1] This mirror is illustrated in *The Dictionary of English Furniture*, 1954, Vol. II, page 312, fig. 5, and both front and back are shown in *From Polished Metal to Looking-Glass*, by Geoffrey Wills, in *Country Life*, Vol. CXXIV No. 3223 (October 23rd, 1958), page 939, figs. 2 and 3.

A Directory of London Makers and Sellers of Looking-glasses

THE list that follows gives particulars of some Londoners who were concerned in making and dealing in looking-glasses and frames, roughly between the years 1670 and 1820. In some instances, little or nothing beyond their names and approximate dates, and occasionally not even their addresses, are known, but, in others, specific work has been attributed to them. More rarely, it is known that they were responsible for the execution of surviving specimens.

It is unlikely that information about most of these men will ever be plentiful. That many famous cabinet-makers have been recorded as supplying looking-glasses at different times cannot be accepted as proof that they were the actual manufacturers of them. Equally because a known man made a particular design it cannot be concluded that he was responsible for an example made to that pattern. In the past, as now, there were more middlemen than makers; and a man who announced that he 'Makes and Sells' could not be taken literally; the word 'Make' was often used loosely, and in many instances 'supply' would have been more accurate.

Practices varied from workshop to workshop, but on the whole carving and gilding were distinct branches of the trade of cabinet-making. Apart from the biggest men, who would have had separate departments of their own for each type of work, frame-making and finishing would have been sub-contracted to those specialising in the craft. Even then, there were further divisions, and some would seem to have made only frames for pictures and prints, while others stated that they framed looking-glasses and a third group did both. Others, again, supplied the plates of glass, ready silvered and ground, to those in the aforementioned trades. To requote von Uffenbach: '. . . the panes are sold to other people who cut and mount them, making mirrors of them; this is a special trade followed by many people in London.' Also, it must be remembered that the word 'frame' was applied to that of a table supporting a marble top, and an eighteenth-century invoice referring to 'a carved frame' is just as likely to be a console or side-table as something for hanging on a wall to enhance a painting or print.

Surviving old looking-glasses are rarely marked in any way that helps to identify their maker. A very few still bear printed labels on their flimsy backboards, but these attractive and informative slips of paper seldom endure the stresses of age. Many have been removed or defaced over the years, and the successive restorations of both frame and glass to which the average looking-glass will have been subjected makes their continued existence highly improbable. The indelible marking of furniture by means of a metal stamp with the maker's name on it was never practised as widely in England as in France and was not used at all for looking-glass frames. Unless a particular piece is documented in some other way there will always be argument as to its authorship.

Much of the information has been gleaned from contemporary Directories. These began to appear in the mid-eighteenth century (there was a sporadic issue in the late seventeenth century, and then no more for fifty years), but it was some time before it became the rule to list other than the most eminent 'Merchants'. At first, craftsmen were ignored, and in many cases only a name and address was listed until it became customary to note a profession, trade or craft against each. There is a happy disregard for accuracy in spelling of both names and addresses, and compilers of Directories were not always to be trusted either for accuracy or honesty. Other sources are Rate Books and, most informative of all but often very elusive, advertisements in newspapers of the time. In addition, the following have been consulted:

Arthur T. Bolton	*The Architecture of Robert and James Adam*, 2 vols., 1922.
Oliver Brackett	*Thomas Chippendale*, n.d. (1924)
Francis Buckley	*Old London Glasshouses*, privately printed, 1915.
	Alphabetical List of Glass Sellers, etc., of London, Recorded in the Newspapers and Other Records Between 1660 and 1800. Unpublished manuscript. (Guildhall MS. 3384.)
Ralph Edwards and Margaret Jourdain	*Georgian Cabinet-Makers*, third edition, 1955.
Ralph Edwards and Percy Macquoid	*The Dictionary of English Furniture*, second edition, revised by Ralph Edwards, 3 vols., 1954.
Celia Fiennes	*Through England on a Side Saddle*, 1880. Reissued as *The Journeys of Celia Fiennes*, edited by Christopher Morris, 1947, revised 1949.
Rupert Gunnis	*Dictionary of British Sculptors, 1660–1851*, 1953.
Albert Hartshorne	*Old English Glasses*, 1897.
Ambrose Heal	*London Furniture Makers, 1660–1840*, 1953.
H. D. Roberts	*History of the Royal Pavilion, Brighton*, 1939.

H. Clifford Smith	*Buckingham Palace*, 1931.
R. W. Symonds	*English Looking-glass Plates and their Manufacture*, in *The Connoisseur*, XCVI (1935) page 315, XCVII (1936) page 243, and XCVIII (1936) page 9.
	Masterpieces of English Furniture and Clocks, 1940.
	Furniture-Making in 17th and 18th Century England, 1940.
G. Scott Thomson	*Family Background* (the Dukes of Bedford at Woburn Abbey and elsewhere), 1949.
Horace Walpole	*A Description of the Villa of Strawberry Hill*, 1774.
	Strawberry Hill Accounts, edited by Paget Toynbee, Oxford, 1927.
P. Ward-Jackson	*English Furniture Designs of the Eighteenth Century*, 1958.
	The Diary of John Hervey, first Earl of Bristol, S.H.A.H. (ed.), Wells, 1894.

THE DIRECTORY

Name and address are given (and trade, if recorded).

Adair, —. Carver and gilder.

Supplied looking-glasses to Sir William Lee, Hartwell House, Bucks., in 1766 and 1778.

Alken, Samuel. Woodcarver.

Carved a looking-glass frame for Sir William Chambers, and subscribed to his *Treatise of Civil Architecture*, 1759.

Allen, —. Upholstery, cabinet and looking-glass manufactory. c. 1800. 21, Little Eastcheap.

Andrews, G. Looking-glass manufactory. 7, Charing Cross.

Recommended by Duncan Macdonald in *The New London Family Cook* (1812).

Angus, Joseph. Looking-glass warehouse. 1790. 18, Aldermanbury.

Arbunot, Jacob. Looking-glass shop. The Royal Cabinet, over against Church Court, Strand.

Newspaper report that he had suffered from fire at his premises: '. . . a great many of his Glasses have been broke, having had not time to move, the Fire being all round him, and a great many lost, as well as many of his Houshold Goods.' Rescues were effected by onlookers, as is made clear by the final paragraph: 'This is therefore to desire any one that has any of his Glasses or Houshold Goods, to return them, and they shall be well Rewarded for their Trouble.' (*The Post Man*, 27 October, 1715.) In the *Daily Post*, 22 March, 1727, he announced that he was 'leaving off Trade, all sorts of Pier Glasses to be sold'.

Arbunot, Philip. Looking-glass shop. Corner of Villiers Street, Strand.

Supplied Queen Anne with 'Two large Sconces wth double Branches, finely gilded, being Three foot deep, scoloped, diamond cutt and engraved, embollished wth crimson and gold Mosaic work wth flowers, on the bodys of the Glass's &c.' These cost £12 7s. and were sent as a gift to the Emperor of Morocco. In the *Daily Courant*, 14 January, 1716, Arbunot announced he was '. . . designing to leave off his Trade: The Goods consisting of all Sorts of Looking-Glasses, Glass Pannels and Sconces . . .'. The *Daily Courant*, 29 April, 1727, announced that he was 'lately deceased' and that his premises were to be let.

Ashlin, William (later trading as Ashlin, Collings & Ashlin). Looking-glass manufactory. 6, Belton Street, Long Acre.

In 1789 estimated the cost of materials for Carlton House (George, Prince of Wales) at £2,500. For the Pavilion, Brighton, supplied the chimney-glass in the Music Room (£701 17s.) (Plate 156) and those in the Banqueting Room (£976 10s.) to the same Royal client. These sums were part of a total of £9,054 5s. 7d. paid to Ashlin and Collings for plate-glass and looking-glass between 1817 and 1823.

Atkinson, Thomas. *The Sun*, south side of St Paul's.
Successor to John Belchier (*q.v.*). His card states: 'Makes & Sells all sorts of Cabinet Work, Chairs, Looking Glasses . . .'.

Ayton, J. *c.* 1790. 73, Berners Street, Oxford Road.
'Sells all sorts of Green and Gold Dressing Glasses, Pier Glasses, Girandoles, etc.'

Bailey, J. Looking-glass-frame-maker. *c.* 1790. Worship Square, Shoreditch.

Bailey & Saunders. Cabinet-makers. *c.* 1820. 13, Mount Street.
The sum of over £15,000 which they were paid for work in the Music Room at the Royal Pavilion, Brighton, included £857 11s. for the chimney-glass.

Beast, William. Looking-glass maker.
The Registers of St Peter Paul's Wharf record the burial of 'Andrew Beast son of William Beast looking glass maker' on 18 February, 1619. The church of St Peter Paul's Wharf, was burned down in the Fire of London in 1666 and was not rebuilt, but the parish was united with St Benet, Paul's Wharf. He may have been an employee of Sir Robert Mansell.

Belchier (or Belcher), **John.** *The Sun*, south side of St Paul's.
Successor to T. Atkinson (*q.v.*). Supplied an over-mantel looking-glass to Mrs Elizabeth Purefoy, Shalstone Manor, Bucks., in 1735. It cost £3 16s. See: G. Eland (Ed.), *The Purefoy Papers*, 2 vols., 1931, plate 10.

Bell, Daniel. Cabinet-maker. St Martin's Lane.
Little is known of this man except that his premises suffered damage by fire in 1728. A few days after the event he announced that he had acquired premises 'opposite to my late Dwelling House'. In 1734 he supplied furniture, including 'a large carved and guilt sconce, pediment frame', to the 'Hon. Counsellor Rider' at Sandon Hall, Staffordshire. (Earl of Harrowby.)

Bell, Henry. *c.* 1740. At the *White Swan* against the South Gate in St Paul's Church Yard.
'Makes & Sells . . . all sorts of Looking Glasses . . . N.B. Old Glasses new Worked & made up Fashionable.'

Bomer, Abraham. Looking-glass maker. *c.* 1709. Bedfordbury, Covent Garden.

Bradburn, John. Cabinet-maker. Hemming's Row, St Martin's Lane, 1758–75; 8, Long Acre, 1767–76.
Succeeded William Vile (*q.v.*) as Cabinet-maker to George III, and made furniture for Buckingham Palace between 1763 and 1776. In 1767 he supplied for Queen Charlotte at St James's Palace, 'A large rich-bordered chimney-glass with rich carved frame gilt in burnish'd gold with 46 brackets for china, with rich festoons of flowers and crown on the top, and 21 panes of looking glass' at a cost of £118. Bradburn died in 1781, and the *Gentleman's Magazine* recorded that he was 'formerly upholsterer to his Majesty, but had retired some years'.

Brewer, James. Carver, gilder and looking-glass manufacturer. *c.* 1784. 33, Snow Hill.

Brewer, Willoughby. Carver, gilder and looking-glass manufacturer. *c.* 1784. 33, Snow Hill.
In 1790 his address was Red Lion Street, Clerkenwell.

Brydon, John. Print seller and Looking-glass manufacturer. *c.* 1785–90. 7, Charing Cross.

Burrough, John. *c.* 1677–90. *The Looking Glass*, Cornhill.
In partnership with William Farnborough (*q.v.*).

Buskin, William. Looking-glass manufacturer. Snow Hill, and later Wellclose Square.
The *London Gazette*, 28th March, 1780, announced that William Buskin was retiring from partnership with Michael Dunn. By 1790 Buskin's address was Wellclose Square and he was trading on his own.

Caddey, John. Cabinet and Looking-glass maker. *The Cabinet*, King Street, the corner of Guildhall Yard, and also in Wood Street.
Newspaper announcements, 1724–7.

Cannon or **Canon, Edward.** 'Paper machée manufacturer.' *c.* 1780. 109, High Holborn.
In 1785 Bailey's *Directory* lists him as 'Paper-hanging and Looking-glass Warehouse', and the *Universal British Directory* five years later as 'Paper machée and Looking-glass Manufacturer'. It would seem that 'Paper-hanging' is a mistake for papier-mâché.

Chabot, Robert. Looking-glass manufacturer. *c.* 1790. 31 Leadenhall Street.

Chippendale, Thomas. Cabinet-maker. *The Chair*, St Martin's Lane.
Thomas Chippendale's name is synonymous in the minds of most people with eighteenth-century English furniture. Born at Otley, Yorkshire, in 1718, he came to London and soon after arriving, having settled even-

tually in St Martin's Lane, published the book of designs, *The Gentleman and Cabinet-Maker's Director*, on which his fame rests. The first two editions of 1754 and 1755 were almost alike, but the third of 1762 was much enlarged and the existence of unpublished designs suggests a fourth was contemplated.

There is no evidence that Chippendale himself actually worked at the bench in London, but his firm was an eminent one for the supply of high quality furniture for the formal rooms of great houses, for curtains and upholstery, and for the simpler requirements of the servants' quarters.

Soon after the issue of the *Director* his business was already on a considerable scale, as the following paragraph from the *Gentleman's Magazine* (April, 1755, Vol. XXV, page 183) makes clear:

Saturday 5

'A fire broke out at the workshop of Mr Chippendale, a cabinet maker near St Martin's Lane, which consumed the same, wherein were the chests of 22 workmen.'

A further report shows that the conflagration was on some subsidiary premises:

'On Saturday Night, at Nine O'Clock, a Fire broke out at a Charcoal Warehouse in the back part of Rose-Street, Covent-Garden, which burnt the said Warehouse, and damaged several Work Houses belonging to divers Persons. M. Roubilliac, the Statuary, has suffered considerably, his Shop being contiguous.' (*General Evening Post*, No. 3322. 5–8th April, 1755.)

The *Director* contains designs for looking-glass frames, and a number resembling them in varying degree have survived. Others exist with Chippendale's original bills, but it is found that these are not confined in pattern to those in the published work and it is known that some were designed by Robert Adam. As there is a lack of evidence to the contrary it is assumed that their carving and gilding was carried out in Chippendale's workshops. Equally, of course, work of this specialised nature could have been sub-contracted, but in view of the substantial size of the business there is a possibility that the invoices can be taken at their face value and the conclusion drawn that they were executed on the premises.

Chippendale gave evidence before the 1773 Parliamentary Committee stating that he dealt in French looking-glass, and that he did so because of its superior size which could not be attained by English makers.

In June, 1769, he had agreed to deliver to Robert Adam 'in about Two months from this Date', for framing by William France (*q.v.*), 'The Following French plate Glass, in London silver'd and ready to be put up.

Two plates 74 ins. by 44 ins. at £69 10 each	£139 0 0
Four Dos. 74 by 26 at £35 each	£140 0 0
Four Dos. 74 by 13 at £15 5 each	£61 0 0
	£340 0 0

In the event, the glass was delivered after the stated time and only after the client, the Earl of Mansfield, had advanced half the agreed amount. The receipt for payment in full was dated 29th November, 1769, and signed by Thomas Chippendale, jr, and William France. The looking-glasses were placed in recesses at either side of the Library fireplace at Kenwood, but were removed later in favour of bookshelves.

Looking-glasses supplied and invoiced by Chippendale are as follows:

1759 The Earl of Dumfries, Dumfries House, Ayrshire. A pair of carved and gilt girandoles.

1766 The Duke of Portland, ?London, Bulstrode or Welbeck. Two very large Oval Glasses with rich carved frames Gilt in burnished Gold, with three branches for candles to each and brass pans [and] Noselles to Ditto £48. It has been suggested that these are two mirrors now in the Victoria and Albert Museum (nos. W2387– and W2388–1855) which were purchased at the Bernal sale in 1855. In the sale there were two pairs of looking-glasses in shaped, carved and gilt frames, each with three candle-arms, but each pair differing slightly in design and size. They were sold singly on the thirtieth day of the sale, lots 4143, 4144, 4149 and 4150, and the predecessor of the museum (the Museum of Ornamental Art, at Marlborough House) bought 4143 for £50 and 4149 for £36 10s. There is no record of where Ralph Bernal obtained them and their noble ancestry, and the identity of their maker is based only on assumption. (Plates 90 and 91.)

1767 Sir Edward Knatchbull, Bt, Mersham Hatch, Kent. A very large Oval Glass in a very rich Carv'd frame partly Gilt & Glass Borders £46

A very large Gerandole richly Carv'd & part Gilt with looking Glass in the Back & three Branches with Brass leaf Nozels £22

A large Oval Glass in a rich Carv'd frame painted Blue and White £23 10

2 Large Gerandoles very richly Carv'd & painted Blue & White with large Looking Glasses in the Backs, 2 Branches to each & Wrought Nozels   £26

2 Gerandoles very neatly Carv'd & part Gilt in Burnished Gold & 2 Branches to each with Leaf nozels & silvering his own Glasses for ditto   £9 9

Making new Backs & feet for 3 Iappan'd Glass frames 2 new Glasses & silvering one your own   £2 15

6 Mahogany dressing frames for your own Glass new silvering the Glasses & a large Glass with a Compas [rounded] Top in a Mahogany frame   £2 15

1772   David Garrick, Esq., Adelphi Terrace, London.
2 very large Peer Glasses in neat Carv'd Frames gilt in Burnished Gold complete   £138

A very Large Rich Carv'd Frame Gilt in burnish'd Gold to your own Glass   £30

4 small Dressing Glasses for Servants   16s.

A new plate of Glass to a Japan Dressing Frame & new Mahoy. frame to part of the old glass 12s.

1773   Edwin Lascelles, Esq. (later Earl of Harewood), Harewood House, Yorkshire.
A very large pier glass   £290

A superb Frame to do. with very large Antique ornaments exceedingly richly Carved and highly finished in Burnished Gold   £70

A fine Looking Glass—91 by 57½   £160

A very large Elegant Frame to do. with Antique Ornaments exceedingly richly carved and highly finished in Burnished Silver with a large Head-plate and broad looking glass borders with 2 paintings on do.—Compleat   £75

1774   Ninian Home, Esq., Paxton House, Berwick-on-Tweed.
A very large oval glass in a carved and gilt frame with ornaments   £16 16s.

2 small swing dressing glasses for servants   10s.

It is known also that Chippendale was responsible for supplying furnishings to Lord Shelburne at Shelburne (later Lansdowne) House in 1772, to John Parker at Saltram, Devonshire, in 1771–2, and to others, but surviving accounts do not detail the items. He was concerned also, in about 1770, with the fitting-up of Carlisle House, Soho Square, for Madame Cornelys, who organised semi-public functions there. Again, it is not known exactly what goods were supplied, but it is not improbable that looking-glasses were amongst them. Certainly there were some in the rooms, for one was smashed when the ingenious Joseph Merlin ran into it while exhibiting his newly-invented roller-skates and did damage estimated at the time at five hundred pounds. Chippendale died in 1779. He was in partnership with James Rannie until 1766 and with Thomas Haig from 1771 until 1779. It is believed that both these men were concerned with giving financial rather than artistic or practical help. The business was carried on until 1796 by Haig and Thomas Chippendale, jr, and until 1821 by the latter. The address remained St Martin's Lane until 1814, was then 57, Haymarket and finally 42, Jermyn Street. (See pages 23–8 and Plates 90, 91, 96 and 140.)

Cole, George. 'Upholder.' Golden Square.

He supplied furniture to Mr Paul Methuen at Corsham Court, Wiltshire, in about 1761, but the items have not been identified as no detailed bills have been found. Some pieces in the house have for long been ascribed to Thomas Johnson (q.v.). In 1761 Cole supplied a pier-glass to the Duke of Atholl at Dunkeld House in Scotland, and in 1763 three similar glasses with side-tables *ensuite* for the Duke's Perthshire seat, Blair Castle. These, again, show close similarities to Johnson's work and have many points in common with his engraved designs, and it has been suggested that Cole employed Johnson to design and execute pieces for which he had obtained orders. (See A. Coleridge: *Chippendale, The Director and some Cabinet-makers at Blair Castle*, in *The Connoisseur*, December, 1960 (Vol. CXLVI, pp. 252–6), and Helena Hayward: *Thomas Johnson and English Rococo*, 1964, pp.36–8.) (Plate 78).

Cooper, George. Looking-glass manufacturer. *c.* 1790. 82, Lombard Street.

Bailey's *Directory* lists him in 1785 as 'Carver and glass-grinder'.

Cooper, Joseph. Looking-glass manufacturer. *c.* 1790. 20 Noble Street.

Cox, Joseph. Frame-maker and gilder. *c.* 1760. Round Court, St Martin's le Grand.

'Makes & Sells all Sorts of Carv'd and Gilt Frames for Looking Glasses . . . Likewise Old Glasses New Silver'd & put into the Newest Fashion Gilt Sconces.'

Cribb, Robert. Glass & Picture frame-maker. *c.*1790. 288, Holborn.

'Old Frames new Gilt & Glasses new Silvered.'

Day, Philip. Carver, gilder and looking-glass manufacturer. *c.* 1784–90. 3, Newgate Street.

Duchemin, Peter. Carver, gilder and looking-glass manufacturer. *c.* 1790. 3, Great Russel Street, Bloomsbury.

Heal lists him with these trades, but his card refers only to the framing of prints and the cleaning of pictures.

Dunn, Michael.
See William Buskin.

Elliot, Richard. Carver and gilder. *c.* 1760. *The Golden Head*, corner of Queen Street, Cheapside.

'. . . Looking Glasses . . are Fram'd or Sold . . .'.

Everidge, John. Looking-glass manufactory. *c.* 1790. Gravel Lane, Southwark.

Farnborough, William. *The Looking Glass*, Cornhill.

Heal gives his dates as 1672–90, spells his name both 'Farmborough' and 'Farnborough', and states that he was in partnership with John Burroughs (*q.v.*). He supplied several looking-glasses to Charles II including one for the lodge at Richmond in 1677.

Faucon, James. Cabinet-maker and glass-grinder. Surman's Great House, Soho Square.

Sale of stock advertised in *The Daily Post*, 15th March, 1731.

Fentham, Thomas. Carver, gilder and frame-maker. 52, Strand (from 1783); 136, Strand (from 1802).

His occupations are given variously in Directories, and a trade-card states 'Carver and glass-grinder'. An oval gilt looking-glass at 10 Downing Street bears his label, and records that he 'sells all sorts of picture, print, and looking-glass frames, of any colour to match rooms'. (Plate 163.)

France, William. Cabinet-maker. St Martin's Lane.

Worked in partnership with Samuel Beckwith for the Crown. Among furniture supplied in 1768–70 for the first Earl of Mansfield at Kenwood, Middlesex, were two looking-glass frames, designed by Robert Adam, at a cost of £149 8s. The glass was imported from France and supplied by Thomas Chippendale (*q.v.*).

Fricker, Thomas. Glass seller. New Street Square, Fetter Lane.

The *Daily Advertiser*, 4th July, 1777, announced that Fricker had ceased to be in partnership with a man named Purcell.

Fricker & Henderson. Paper-hanging Warehouse. 161, New Bond Street.

This firm executed carving and gilding at the Royal Pavilion, Brighton, *c.* 1820. It included: Music Room, £1321 1 1od.; Saloon, more than £3,000; and Banqueting Room, £7,944 8 2d., the latter including £216 18s. for the chimney glasses. Between 1820 and 1823 Henderson alone was paid £1,035 for work done on looking-glasses in the Pavilion. Directories during the first decade of the nineteenth century list the firm as above, later there is a 'Jas Henderson, Paper-hanging Manufacturer' at 80, New Bond Street, who may or may not be the Henderson concerned.

Gates, William. Cabinet-maker. Long Acre.

He was cabinet-maker to George III from 1777, and his identified work includes some inlaid commodes of high quality. In 1781 he supplied the Prince of Wales (later Prince Regent and George IV) with: 'a chimney glass in a carved frame with fine top to do., with clusters of flowers hanging in festoons from vases and other ornaments and husks down the two sides of the frame, all very richly gilt in burnished gold; a large plate in the middle and borders to do. Size of the frame 7 ft. 7 in. wide.' The charge was £63.

Gilbert, John. Carver. Mount Street, Golden Square.

Is known to have supplied eight looking-glasses for the Mansion House, London, in 1752. Between 1767 and 1768 he provided 'a large glass frame with ornaments at top and bottom' for Lord Shelburne (Lansdowne House). A John Gilbert who was at Great Queen Street from 1732 to 1768 is described as 'Upholder to His Majesty', but it is uncertain whether he is the same man or a namesake.

Goodison, Benjamin. Cabinet-maker. *The Spread Eagle*, Long Acre.

Supplied royalty and the nobility between about 1727 and 1767. He made 'three glass sconces in carved and gilt frames, with two wrought arms each' for the Prince of Wales in 1732–3, which are now in Hampton Court Palace. For the same patron he made 'A large pier glass in a tabernacle frame gilt' at a cost of £50. A looking-glass in the Victoria and Albert Musem (W. 86–1911) was probably made by Goodison also for the

Prince, as the cresting incorporates his badge of three ostrich feathers encircled by a coronet. He worked also for the Earl of Leicester (Holkham), the first and second Viscounts Folkestone (Longford Castle), the Duke of Newcastle, and perhaps also the Earl of Harrington. Goodison died in 1767. (Plates 54 and 62.)

Gough, James. Carver, gilder and maker of composition ornaments. c. 1790. 219, Piccadilly.

Gould, William. Glass-cutter and looking-glass maker. 78, Gracechurch Street.

Trading as follows: William Gould, 1790; Thomas Gould & Co., 1798; Wm. Gould & Son, 1799.

Greene, John. Glass seller. *King's Arms*, Poultry.

Greene imported glass of all kinds from Venice. In a letter written by him in London to Antonio Morelli in Venice, dated 10th February, 1670/71, is the request: 'That the Lookeing Glasses be all verry good Cleer whit Mettle and Cleer and free from Bladders or great Sands or any other Blemishes or faults what soe ever, and that they be Large size for the sortt for many of ye Last you sent wear much under size.' (See page 43, footnote 4).

Gumley, John. Cabinet-maker and looking-glass manufacturer. Salisbury Exchange and the corner of Norfolk Street, Strand; New Exchange, Strand, from 1714.

John Gumley is remembered by numerous reports in newspapers in his day, and because he was eulogised in print by Steele. He set up a glasshouse at Lambeth in 1705 (see page 46), and supplied looking-glasses to royalty and the nobility. One, at Hampton Court Palace, bears his name in raised letters on a gilt slip across an intersection of two panels of glass, and another, at Chatsworth, has scratched on it 'John Gumley 1703' (Plate 20). For it and its companion the Duke of Devonshire paid £200. Gumley was in partnership with James Moore from 1714 to 1726, and with William Turing from 1727 until his death in 1729. His business was then continued by his mother, Elizabeth Gumley, and Turing, but royal patronage was withdrawn from them 'on account of their notorious impositions'. (Plates 20, 22 and 22a.)

Hallet (or **Hallett**) **William.** Cabinet-maker. Great Newport Street (1732–53); St Martin's Lane (1753–69).

A fashionable and eminent cabinet-maker who numbered many of the nobility among his patrons. He achieved sufficient financial success to purchase in 1745 the former estate of the Duke of Chandos, Canons, at Whitchurch, Middlesex. There he built himself a home and was painted by Francis Hayman, R.A., in a family group with himself in the centre grasping in his hand a plan of the house. Horace Walpole employed Hallet on one occasion for the supply of furnishings for Strawberry Hill. The total sum involved was £73 11 4d., which included £13 'for black frames to Gothic glasses'. (See Plate 138.)

Hancock, Colebron. Glass-cutter. Hedge Lane, Charing Cross (later renamed Whitcomb Street).

J. T. Smith in *Nollekens and His Times* noted that the premises used by William Wilton (*q.v.*) were later occupied 'by a glass manufacturer of the name of Hancock, for whom Doctor Johnson wrote a hand-bill'. He was a cutter of glass other than looking-glass, and there would seem to be no record of Dr Johnson having had any connection with him or his business activities. Hancock did supply some table-glass to another famous writer, the historian Edward Gibbon.

Hancox, Nicholas. Glass-grinder. Belton Street, opposite Brownlow Street, Long Acre.

'Hancox & Co, looking-glass men' were owed the sum of £2337 13 2d. for work at, and goods supplied to, Carlton House for the Prince of Wales between 1783 and 1786. By 1790 he was recorded as being in business at Castle Street, Long Acre.

Hartley, Thomas. Carver and gilder. c. 1790–94. 108, Newgate Street.

'Performs all manner of house & furniture Carving, &c. Looking Glasses & frames for Exportation.'

Hawkins, H. Looking-glass and frame-maker. c. 1760. Compton Street, Soho.

Holmes, Richard. Cabinet-maker and glass-grinder. c. 1783. *The Tea Chest*, 22 Barbican.

'Makes all Sorts of Looking Glasses in Carved and Mahogany Frames . . . N.B. Old Glasses New Framed & Silvered.'

Horne, Abial. Cabinet-maker and glass-grinder. c. 1768–83. 19, Wellclose Square.

'Sells all Sorts of Looking Glasses . . . at the Lowest Prices. N.B. For Exportation.'

Howcraft, Thomas. Cabinet-maker. *The Looking Glass*, Cornhill; *The India Cabinet*, Long Acre (from 1711).

In partnership with Richard Robinson (*q.v.*) supplied looking-glasses to the Earl of Nottingham at

Burley-on-the-Hill, Rutland, in 1711. One of them cost £82 1 6d., which included patterned and scalloped glass borders and a cut coat of arms in the shaped top panel. (Plate 21.)

Hudgebout, James. Glass-grinder and cabinet seller. *The Looking Glass*, Cornhill.

Succeeded John Burrough (q.v.) at this address, and recorded as 'leaving off trade' in 1704.

Hudson, George.

Supplied Charles II with two looking-glasses 25 in. in length described at the time as 'large'.

Hudson, Stephen (or **Solomon?**). Carver and gilder. In business 1770–93. 16, Titchfield Street, Cavendish Square.

Supplied pier-glasses to the Earl of Buckinghamshire, Blickling Hall, Norfolk.

Iden, Henry. Looking-glass seller. Ludgate Street.

Announced in the *London Gazette*, 16 February, 1688, that he was 'leaving off trade'.

Ince, William and John Mayhew. Cabinet-makers. *c.* 1759–83. Broad Street, Golden Square.

This firm is known principally from its publication of a book of furniture designs: *The Universal System of Household Furniture*, issued in shilling parts between 1759 and 1762, and in a single volume probably in the latter year. Kent's *Directory for the Year 1780* lists 'Mayhew & Ince, Cabinet-makers, Upholders, & Dealers in Plate Glass, 20, Marshall-street, Carnaby Market', and a more interesting entry in the *Universal British Directory* ten years later seems to have escaped notice: it lists their trades as 'Upholders, Cabinet-makers and Manufacturers of Plate Glass'. The connection with glass receives verification from the fact that a 'Mr John Mayo, a Cabinet Maker and Worker of Plate Glass' gave evidence before the Parliamentary Committee of 1773 (see page 132). There can be no doubt that in spite of the phonetic spelling of his name, this man was John Mayhew. 'Mayo's' trade of 'Worker of Plate Glass' is not easy to define; it could mean that he merely dealt in the material or that he ground, polished and silvered glass made elsewhere. There is no suggestion in his evidence that he actually had a glassworks of his own, but it is quite possible that he had started one by 1790, seventeen years later, when the *Directory* was issued.

Productions of the firm that have been identified are few in number, but some looking-glass frames made to

designs in their *Universal System* are known, and they also executed work for Robert Adam. (See pp. 30–1 and Plates 97 and 151.) *See* MAYHEW, John.

Jenson or **Johnson, Gerrit** or **Gerreit.** Cabinet-maker and Glass seller. St Martin's Lane.

Served the Royal Household during the reigns of Charles II, James II, William and Mary, and Queen Anne, and supplied furnishings for Kensington Palace which included overmantels and pier-glasses. He worked also at Chatsworth for the Duke of Devonshire, and provided much of the window glass for the mansion. In 1692 Jensen made for the 'great chamber' a door containing panes of looking-glass, which was seen by Celia Fiennes soon after its installation. She wrote of 'a Large door all of Looking glass in great pannells all diamond Cutt', but the 'pannells' were replaced in the nineteenth century by a single sheet of looking-glass.

In 1696 the first Earl of Bristol noted in his Diary: 'Paid Mr Gerreit Johnson yᵉ Cabinet-maker in full of his bill for yᵉ black sett of Glass, table & stands, & for yᵉ glasses, etc., over yᵉ chimneys & elsewhere in dear wife's apartment, £70.' In the same year he supplied William III with '8 Large glasse Ovall Sconces with two branches the frames glasse' at a cost of £80.

In the *Daily Courant*, 2nd May, 1715, it was announced that 'Mr Johnson, Cabinet-Maker to her late Majesty Queen Anne', had retired from business and had for sale, *inter alia*, 'several very large Looking-Glasses in Glass Frames, and other Glasses, Chimney-Glasses and Sconces'.

Johnson, Robert. Carver and gilder. *The Golden Head*, Frith Street, Soho.

His trade-card of about 1760 states that he 'Makes all Sorts of . . . Glass Sconce Frames . . .'.

Johnson, Thomas. Carver and teacher of drawing and modelling. Queen Street, Seven Dials—to *c.* 1757; *The Golden Boy*, Grafton Street, Soho—from about 1757.

In 1758 he published a book of patterns: *Twelve Girandoles*, and three years later issued in monthly parts a set of designs eventually published as *One Hundred and Fifty New Designs*. Some of these were reprinted in the nineteenth century with the name of the draughtsman removed and that of Chippendale substituted.

The following have been identified as being of Johnson's designing, and may have been made by him: a pair of large looking-glasses of carved and stained deal, and a pair of girandoles of carved and painted deal, at Hagley Hall, Worcestershire; a pair of oval gilt-framed looking-glasses, at Corsham Court, Wiltshire; and an overmantel looking-glass, in the Victoria and Albert Museum, London. Some pier-glasses at Blair Castle, Perthshire, have been ascribed to Johnson as they are in his manner. They were supplied by George Cole (*q.v.*), but he may well have been only an inter-mediary, and as he was also the supplier of the glasses at Corsham (noted above), it is not improbable that Johnson carried out orders for him. (See pages 29 and 141 and Plates 78, 88 and 89.)

Jones, Thomas. Looking-glass seller. *Seven Stars*, St Paul's Churchyard.

In *The Daily Post* for 29th November, 1725, he announced that he had 'left off business'.

Jouret, Henry. Carver and gilder. *c.* 1770. *The Archi-trave Frame*, Grafton Street, Soho; *The Gold Frame*, Maiden Lane, Covent Garden.

A trade-card giving the second address states: 'Makes all Sorts of Black and Gold Frames for Paintings, Prints, and Glasses, and all sorts of Ornaments Carved and Gilded.' It is signed *M. Lock Fecit*.

Kemp, George. Cabinet-maker. *The Golden Ball*, 64, Cornhill.

George Kemp was at this address from about 1760 to 1790, and Matthew Kemp, probably his son, from 1792 to 1814. Heal reproduces his trade-card of about 1760 on which he 'makes and sells' cabinet goods and looking-glasses. In a 1783 directory his occupation is given as 'upholsterer and glass-grinder', which links him and Matthew Kemp with a petition presented to the House of Commons in April, 1794, respecting the affairs of the Plate Glass Company at Ravenhead. Four years prior, the Company had 'agreed to provide for Messieurs Kemp all Materials and Things needful for building a Mill or Mills, according to their said Secret or Invention' for polishing and grinding plate glass. Identification is confirmed in the Parliamentary records where the Christian names of the two men are given. Heal gives also George Kemp & Son at 64, Leadenhall Street in 1790–93, but this may be a contemporary error.

Keylock, John. Looking-glass manufacturer. *c.* 1790. 11, Hatton Garden.

Knapton, Samuel. Looking-glass seller. Great Queen Street, St Giles's.

Knapton was Master of the Glass-Sellers' Company in 1712. The *General Advertiser* for 11th October, 1736, mentioned: 'Samuel Knapton, a looking-glass seller, died on the 12th December, 1720, aged 47.'

Lecand, Benjamin L. Carver and gilder. 38, Great Prescot Street, Goodmansfields.

His early 19th-century trade-card reads: 'B. L. Lecand, Carver, Gilder, Paper Hanger, Looking Glass and Pic-ture Frame Manufacturer, No 38, Great Prescot Street, Goodmansfields. All sorts of Elegant and Ornamental Convex Glasses, &c., in the present Fashion & on the most reasonable terms. Old Frames re-gilt and Paintings carefully cleaned and varnished. Stationery, Book-Binding &c.'. This is reproduced by Ada Polak: *Norwegian Taste in English Art* in *Connoisseur Year Book*, 1959, page 74, together with one of a pair of convex glasses bearing Lecand's card in the Norsk Folke-museum, Oslo.

Leigh, Robert. Cabinet-maker. Bedford Street, Covent Garden.

The first Earl of Bristol recorded in his Diary: '1727. May 13. Paid Robert Leigh ye Cabinet-maker in full for putting in new glasses to ye silver sconces, & India cutt jappan frame, & for a dumb waiter, £10 10s.'

Linnell, James. Carver, gilder, picture-frame maker and print seller. 14, Craven Buildings (1790); 2, Streat-ham Street, Bloomsbury.

Father of the artist, John Linnell. A looking-glass in a carved and gilt frame of Neo-classical design, at 10, Downing Street, bears his name and Bloomsbury address on a label 'written in faded ink'.

Linnell, William and John. Cabinet-makers and carvers. 28, Berkeley Square.

The relationship between these two men and James Linnell, above, is not yet known. William was ap-prenticed to Michael Savidge for seven years from 16th July, 1717, and was free of the Joiners' Company in 1729. He furnished houses in London and elsewhere. After his death in 1763 his stock was sold by auction, and included 'magnificent large Pier and other glasses . . . and girandoles'. He was succeeded by John, his son or nephew, whose fame is assured by the fact that many of his surviving drawings, which are in the Victoria and Albert Museum, have enabled some of his work to be identified. He provided furniture for Shardeloes, Bucks., Kedleston, Derbyshire, Osterley, Middx. and elsewhere, and his clients included many of the nobility of his time. He died in 1796. (Plates 128, 145 and 154.)

Lock, Matthias. Carver. Nottingham Court, Castle Street, Long Acre (1746); near *The Swan*, Tottenham Court Road (1752).

One of the most gifted English designers of his time, he was active between 1740 and 1770, but nothing is known of his career for certain. It has been suggested that he was working for Chippendale from about 1752 until 1769. He issued a number of books of engraved designs in the rococo style including some for sconces, girandoles and looking-glasses. His *New Book of Pier-Frames* of 1769 shows that he was able to adapt himself to the more restrained manner of Robert Adam. Many of his original drawings are in the Victoria and Albert Museum, London, and others are in the Metropolitan Museum, New York. (See pages 23–31 and Plates 60, 61 and 94.) A 1790 Directory lists a Matthias Lock, carver and gilder, at 19, Clerkenwell Green.

Mayhew, John.

In partnership for a period with James Whittle (*q.v.*), but from 1759 with William Ince (*q.v.*).

M'Ewen, John. Looking-glass warehouse. *c.* 1790. Queen Street, Southwark.

Minshall, John. Carver and gilder.

Commenced in Dock Street in 1769, and six years later advertised from *The Golden Key*, Hanover Square, 'an elegant assortment of looking-glasses in oval and square frames, ditto mahogany. Any lady or gentleman who has glass in old-fashioned frames may have these cut into ovals or any pattern desired. The above frames may be finished white or green and white, purple, or any other colour that suits the furniture of the room, or gilt in oil or burnished gold.'

Moore, James. Carver, gilder and cabinet-maker. Short's Gardens, St Giles's.

Moore was in partnership with John Gumley (*q.v.*) from 1714. He specialised in furniture fashionably decorated with carved and gilded gesso, and there are a number of surviving tables in this manner with his name incised on them. In 1710 the Earl of Bristol noted: 'Paid for James Moore in full of his bill for glass peers, sconces, etc., £33 10s.' He worked also for the Court, for the Duke of Montagu at Boughton, for John Mellor of Erthig, and for Sarah, Duchess of Marlborough. For the latter he supplied looking-glasses, and was employed by her first as 'glass man' and later as Clerk of the Works at Blenheim; being referred to by the Duchess as 'my oracle, Mr Moore'. At Erthig, Denbigh-shire, are some looking-glasses supplied by Moore in the years 1724-6, and for which the accounts are reprinted by Edwards and Jourdain: *Georgian Cabinet-Makers*, 1955, p. 116–17. Moore died in 1726, and his stock was advertised to be sold in *The Daily Post*, 1st July, 1728. (Plate 27.)

Neptune, —. Looking-glass seller. Little Queen Street.

His name, trade and address were mentioned in *The Post Man*, 26th May, 1702.

Nodes, William. The Crown, Fleet Ditch.

On 5th November, 1696, the first Earl of Bristol paid Nodes £6 'for 2 looking glasses'.

Norman, Samuel. Cabinet-maker, carver and gilder. King Street, Covent Garden, to late 1759; Soho Square, after 1759 to *c.* 1765.

Norman was in partnership with James Whittle (*q.v.*) for some years and also for a short period with John Mayhew (*q.v.*). Mortimer's *Universal Director* of 1763 refers to him as 'Sculptor and Carver to their Majesties and Surveyor of the curious Carvings in Windsor Castle'. The King Street premises were burned down in December, 1759, and, in the same year, Mayhew terminated his partnership. Norman's address then became 'The Royal Tapestry Manufactory', Soho Square; a business conducted by the last important English weaver, Paul Saunders, who combined this activity with the sale of furniture and fabrics.

In 1759 the Duke of Bedford was supplied with a looking-glass for the State Bedchamber at Woburn Abbey. The account was as follows: 'For making and carving that exceeding large and grand oval frame, with eagles, a shield and rich "Saggs", festoons of flowers twisting round, "Floras" head top and rich flowers curiously finished and gilt in burnish gold complete £97 10s. For a plate of best glass to ditto 49 by 38 complete £65 3s.' During the following year the Duke was charged 18s. for 'white laping and silvering a glass 43 by 25': i.e., repolishing and resilvering a plate. Also in 1760 the Duke paid William Norman, probably a relative, the sum of £229 for '2 large frames in burnished gold' and £183 5s. for 'a plate of glass' (76 by 44). In connection with this transaction there is preserved a valuation of both frames and glass signed by Thomas Woodin and Paul Saunders, which, in view of the connection between the latter and Norman, is perhaps an odd document. At the same time, Samuel Norman receipted the bill and guaranteed to supply a plate of glass within six months to match the one for which the Duke had paid him. (Plate 115.)

Owen, Thomas. Cabinet-maker and glass-grinder. *c.* 1736. Near Moorfields.

Patrick, John. Barometer-maker. Ship Court, Old Bailey.

Patrick was among the first to make the Diagonal, Yard Arm or Signpost barometer invented in 1670 by Sir Samuel Morland. A contemporary writer noted of his instruments: 'And in a Diagonal one (which he very handsomly fits about the Frame of a large Looking-glass, with a Thermometer also by it) the Mercury rises and falls near 30 inches; and consequently, the changes of the Weather will be much sooner perceptable in these Instruments, than in the Barometers of the common form' (J. Harris, *Lexicon Technicum*, 1704). Patrick himself pointed out a further advantage: 'Ladies and gentlemen at the same time they dress may accommodate their habit to the weather—an invention not only curious but also profitable and pleasant.' Examples are very rare to-day, but in 1710 Conrad von Uffenbach recorded seeing one and noted that it cost fifteen guineas. (Plate 9.)

Phillips and Co. Looking-glass manufactory. *c.* 1790. 3, Newgate Street.

Phillips, John. Looking-glass maker. *The Cabinet,* Cornhill.

Mentioned in the *Craftsman* of 12th February, 1732.

Quintin & Windle. Glass-makers. 106, East Smithfield.

A trade-card of about 1760 is headed 'Weatherby, Crowther, Quintin & Windle's Manufactory at the Green Yard, near East Smithfield', and illustrates a number of glass articles: a chandelier, candle-shades, drinking-glasses, etc. Weatherby and Crowther had a better-known connection with the Bow porcelain works in Essex and their London showroom in Cornhill. (See *The Bow Factory under Alderman Arnold and Thomas Frye*, by Hugh Tait in *Trans. English Ceramic Circle*, vol. 5, part 4 (1963), pages 195–216.) Richard Windle was one of the arbitrators appointed following the bankruptcy of John Crowther in 1763, and Thomas Quintin was involved in litigation in 1756, in company with others, regarding the bankruptcy of John Stott, master of the ship *Antelope*, in which they had been concerned

The style of the glass-making firm changed with the years.

1781 Thomas Quintin & Co.
1786 Thomas Quintin & Son.

1799–1810 Quintin & Son, the London Plate Glass Co.
1815 Macnamara & Brett.

Thomas Quintin gave evidence before the Parliamentary Committee of 1773 and stated that he had made very few glass plates, the largest being 84 by 38 ins., and that he had never sold one. He could cast plates, 'but not in the Manner they do in France'.

Rackstrow, Benjamin. Cabinet-maker and sculptor. *The Crown and Looking Glass,* St Martin's Lane, about 1720; *Sir Isaac Newton's Head,* Crane Court, Fleet Street.

A trade-card with the St Martin's Lane address states that Rackstrow 'Makes and Sells all sorts of Cabinet Work, Looking Glasses, Coach glasses, Window Blinds . . . He likewise cleans and repairs all sorts of Cabinet work, Exchanges New Glasses for Old ones and makes Old ones fashionable.' The second address is on a trade-card (this and above *repr.* Heal) dated 1738 and signed by the engraver and furniture designer, Henry Copland. It is worded similarly to the preceding. Rackstrow exhibited at his Fleet Street premises a collection of 'natural and artificial curiosities and anatomical figures'. He received £3 13s. for two busts supplied to the Ironmongers' Company in 1750, and in 1763 exhibited some of his work at the Free Society. It included a bust of 'mr Frye', probably Thomas Frye, the engraver and painter, and arcanist at the Bow china works who had died in the previous year. The *London Magazine* reported the death of Benjamin Rackstrow on 29th May, 1772. It is possible that two men, perhaps father and son, have been confused here.

Richardson, James. Birchin Lane. *c.* 1748.

Listed by Heal as 'Glass and Cabinet-maker'.

Robinson, Richard. Looking-glass maker. The *Flower Pot,* Beaufort Street, Strand.

In 1698 he advertised in the *London Gazette* that he had obtained a patent for a machine by which glass might be ground and the 'borders cut more curiously hollow and better than any heretofore done'. In partnership with Thomas Howcraft (*q.v.*) Robinson supplied looking-glasses to the Earl of Nottingham in 1711. In the previous year he had advertised the disposal of his stock ('no more of the Engine-Work to be had after this Sale'), but the glasses sent to the Earl were probably made prior to this event.

Rogers, Thomas. Strand.

A Patent (No. 1568) was granted to Thomas Rogers on 7th November, 1786, for 'A new method of ornamenting looking-glasses, picture-frames and other kinds of furniture, with carved and moulded glass in relief, plain or coloured;—applicable to many other purposes.'

Rose, S. Looking-glass maker. *c.* 1790. 29, Hog Lane, Shoreditch.

Rose, William. Looking-glass and cabinet-maker. *c.* 1800. 12, Old Street.

Sargent, George. Pier-glass and cabinet-maker. *c.* 1790. 17, College Hill.

Seddon, George or **Seddon, Sons & Shackleton** (after about 1790). Cabinet-makers. Aldersgate Street.

The firm was founded in the mid-eighteenth century by George Seddon. In 1768 the *Gentleman's Magazine* recorded (Vol. XXXVIII, p. 347):

'Thursday 14 [July]. A dreadful fire burnt down London House, formerly the residence of the bishops of London, in Aldersgate-street, now occupied by Mr Seddon, one of the most eminent cabinet-makers in London. The damage is computed at 20,000 £.'

By 1786 the manufacture, cutting and silvering of cast plate glass were included among the activities of the firm (see page 58), but no looking-glasses made by Seddons have yet been identified.

Short, Robert. Cabinet and looking-glass warehouse. Fore Street, near Cripplegate.

His trade-card of *c.* 1780 states that he 'Makes & Sells all Sorts of Looking Glass & Cabinet Work which he Manufactures himself to supply Merchants for Exportation or Home Consumption, on the most reasonable Terms'.

Sibthorpe, Christopher. Aldermanbury.

A Philadelphia goldsmith, Francis Richardson, noted in his account book that he should visit 'Cristepher Siphtha, a Looking Glass maker, at the Sign Looking Glass in Aldermondary', when in London in 1719. Heal gives Sibthorpe's trade as 'Cabinet-maker', and his sign as *The Japan'd Cabinet. See* TANTUM, Joseph.

Simons, John. Looking-glass manufactory. *c.* 1790. 12, Charterhouse Square.

Staunton, —. Looking-glass seller. Moorfields.
Mentioned in the *British Journal*, 21st February, 1730.

Stephens, —. Looking-glass maker. Between *The White Bear* and *The Golden Sugar Loaf*, Long Acre.
Mentioned in *The Post Man*, 18th July, 1702.

Stinton, —. Looking-glass maker. *c.* 1730. Moorfields.

Styfield, Thomas. Carver and glass-grinder. *c.* 1790–93. 35, Old Compton Street.

Tantum, Joseph. Cabinet-maker. Gravel Lane, Houndsditch.

Francis Richardson, a Philadelphia goldsmith, purchased from Tantum in 1719 '20 Looking Glasses'. He recorded this transaction in his account book preserved in the Downs Manuscript Library, Winterthur Museum, Wilmington, Delaware.

Thornton, Christopher. Looking-glass seller. Peter Street, the Mint, Southwark; later in Piccadilly.

A handbill of about 1707 states: 'At Christopher Thornton's living, in *Peterstreet* in the *Mint* in Southwark, at the *Looking-Glass* near the *Square*, are now to be Sold all sorts of Looking-Glasses, Sconces, Chimney-Pieces, Pannel-Glasses, very reasonably, or may change your old Looking-Glasses for new ones, or if you have any old Looking-Glasses that want Silvering, shall be done very reasonably. You may also be furnished with Chests of Drawers, or Looking-Glasses at any price, paying for them Weekly, as we shall agree. Coach Glasses whole Fore-Glass 4*l.* Door-glass 1*l.* a Fore-Glass 8*s.* Pray take care of this Bill.' Thornton does not suggest that he was actually the maker of either glass or frames, but he seems to have been early in the field for supplying furniture on weekly payments.

In 1720 a notice in the *Weekly Journal* gave his address as Piccadilly, and later still he was at *The Cabinet*, Germain (Jermyn) Street: these might have been the same premises with an entrance to each thoroughfare. He announced in *The Daily Post* in 1731 (No. 3793) that he was retiring from business.

Thornton, Christopher. Glass-grinder.
The London Gazette, 17th May, 1743, records that a man of this name and trade was committed to prison for debt.

Turing, William. Looking-glass and cabinet-maker. *The Eagle and Child*, Bedford Street.

Was in partnership with John Gumley (*q.v.*) from 1721, and from 1723–6 his address was 'over against the New Exchange' in the Strand. In *The London Gazette*, 26th January, 1723, he is recorded as Bankrupt, and in *The Daily Post*, 13th April, 1726, announced that he had resumed business in the Strand.

Twaddel, William. Glass-grinder. Hanover Street, Long Acre.

In 1769 supplied eighteen plates of looking-glass,

$27\frac{1}{4}$ by $17\frac{1}{2}$ inches, to Robert Adam for use at Kenwood, Middlesex. The receipted bill for £19 7s. is dated 10th February, 1770.

Vardy, Thomas. Carver. Park Street, Grosvenor Square.

Mentioned in the Will of the architect, John Vardy, dated 13th April, 1762. The two were perhaps related and may have collaborated in designing and making frames. (See Anthony Coleridge, *John Vardy and the Hackwood Suite*, in the *Connoisseur*, Vol. CXLIX, page 12. January, 1962.) He is listed as a carver in Mortimer's *Universal Director*, 1763. (Plate 65.)

Vile, William. Cabinet-maker. 72, St Martin's Lane.

Worked in partnership with John Cobb, but Vile alone supplied furniture to the Royal Family. Some of his work remains at Buckingham Palace and is authenticated by the distinctive design, high quality of timber and craftsmanship, and by surviving details of accounts. In 1763 he regilded and japanned some looking-glass frames of earlier date, so they would match their surroundings in Queen Charlotte's Japan Room; one of these remains at the Palace. (See H. C. Smith, *op. cit.*, plate 230.)

Welch, James. Glass-grinder and looking-glass maker. Behind *The Rose and Crown*, Broadway, Blackfriars.

Advertised in *The Daily Courant*, 29th July, 1724: 'you may be furnished Wholesale or Retale with great Variety of Peer, Chimney or Sconce Glasses, fine Dressing-Glasses, Coach, Chariot, or Chair-Glasses, with Plate Sash-Glasses, &c. N.B. Merchants, Shopkeepers, or Country Chapmen may be furnished with the aforementioned Goods, as also all sorts of small Glasses at the lowest Rates. Old Glasses cleaned or made into new Fashions.'

Whittle, James. Carver and gilder. King Street, Covent Garden.

The architect, Matthew Brettingham, stated that Whittle carved the frames of the pier-glasses in the Drawing-room and the South Dining-room at Holkham House, Norfolk. He supplied looking-glass frames to the Earl of Cardigan in 1742-3, and in partnership with Samuel Norman (*q.v.*) was employed by the Duke of Bedford at Bedford House, London, and at Woburn Abbey, Bedfordshire.

Wilkinson, Thomas. Looking-glass maker. *c.* 1725. Stonecutter Street, near Fleet Ditch.

Wilton, William. Papier-mâché maker. Hedge Lane, Charing Cross, and Edward Street, Cavendish Square.

J. T. Smith opens his Life of Joseph Wilton, R.A., the sculptor (1722–1803), by stating 'he was the son of a plasterer, who, by a vast increase of income, arising principally from a manufactory, in imitation of that in France, for making the *papier-mâché* ornaments for chimney-pieces, and frames for looking-glasses, was enabled to rebuild his premises on the south-west corner of Hedge-lane, Charing-cross; at the same time enlarging his workshops on the west side of Edward-street, Cavendish-square, where his ornamental works were carried on.' (*See also* HANCOCK, and pages 138–9.)

Wood, Stephen. Cabinet-maker. *c.* 1725. *The Cabinet*, near the Bridge foot, Southwark.

'Makes and Sells all Sorts of Cabinet work, Looking Glasses, Peer Glasses and Sconces . . . N.B. Old Glasses mended or Alter'd.'

Wright, S. Carver, gilder and looking-glass manufacturer. *c.* 1830. 388, Strand.

Wyatt, Edward. Carver, gilder and picture-frame maker. 360, Oxford Street.

In 1811, the first year of the Regency, Wyatt executed work at Carlton House for which he charged £756. In 1794 he supplied 'one large chimney-glass frame' and other carving for Lichfield House, 15, St James's Square, which was being decorated by the architect, James Wyatt, for Thomas Anson. It is not improbable that the two men, carver and architect, were related. The 1825 *Post Office London Directory* lists him as 'carver and Gilder to his Majesty', and still at 360, Oxford Street.

Yardley, George. Carver and gilder. *c.* 1770. Noble Street, near Aldersgate.

Young, Lake. Glass seller. *The Coach and Looking Glass* Manufactory, James Street, Covent Garden, and near The Pump, Watling Street.

His card, of about 1760, states: 'Where Merchants, Captains of Ships, Country Chapmen &c, may be supply'd on reasonable Terms with all Sorts of Looking Glasses, Viz^t. Sconce, Pier & Chimney Glasses, Dressing Boxes & Swingers, in Mahogany, Walnut-tree, & Painted, or in rich Carv'd & Gilt Frames, in the neatest Taste & Newest fashion.'

He was a member of the Court of Common Council of the city of London, one of the eight men representing Cordwainer Ward, and was elected in 1768 one of the Commissioners of Sewers, Lamps and Pavements. He is listed in 1769 as one of the twenty-four Directors of the Laudable Society for the Benefit of Widows.

A Directory of 1783 gives Young's trade as 'glass cutter', and his address as 54, Watling Street.

Index

Names of makers and sellers of looking-glasses listed in the Directory (pages 147–158) are not included in the Index except when they are mentioned elsewhere in the book. Figures in bold type refer to the pages on which there are plates.